Baby
Names

NO NONSENSE
PARENTING GUIDE

Baby
Names

BY
PHILIP HARRISON
AND ROSE LEWIS

Longmeadow Press

Cover photography by Marty Czamanske.
Cover design by Bud Lavery/
Ross Culbert Holland & Lavery, Inc.
Production services by William S. Konecky Associates, New York.

Published for Longmeadow Press, 201 High Ridge Road,
Stamford, Connecticut 06904. No part of this book may
be reproduced or used in any form or by any means,
electronic or mechanical, including photocopying,
recording, or by any information storage and retrieval
system, without permission in writing from the publisher.

No Nonsense Parenting Guide is a trademark
controlled by Longmeadow Press.

ISBN: 0-681-40094-3

Printed in the United States of America

9 8 7 6 5 4 3 2

To our dear friends
Brian David, Vivian Florence,
Jason Todd and Jessica Maud Wolfson,
with love

Introduction

A good name is rather to be chosen than great riches. — Proverbs 22:1

YOUR BABY'S FIRST GIFT

The name you select is the first gift you will give your baby. It is also one of your first important parenting responsibilities. You want to be sure of the name you choose. Remember that this gift is meant to last a lifetime.

A name creates a first impression for others, often giving clues as to personality, national origin, and possibly religion. According to psychologists, the name you select may influence how your child feels about him/herself. Consequently, the choice of a name is not to be undertaken lightly. You should consider carefully before you make your final choice.

Let us set out some *No Nonsense* guidelines to help you with this important decision. The first and most important of all is— think!

THINK!

Names are too often chosen on a moment's impulse or because of some temporary attraction. The name you select shouldn't be cute, silly or comical. Your child will have to wear this name every day of his/her life. Granted, we have all heard of people named Bowand Arrow, Hardas Nails, Candy Lane or Ima Hogg, but do you really want to impose that kind of burden on your baby?

1

So the first rule is to take time to think. Remember that the name you select for your baby today may someday be the name of a great scientist, author, attorney, doctor or astronaut—or simply of a full-grown woman or man deeply loved by his/her family. Baby naming is a serious responsibility.

MEANING

Always consider the meaning of the name you select. Someday your child may look it up. Often parents tend toward names of religious, historic, or popular significance. Names of famous actors or statesmen are sometimes selected because parents admire the namesakes. *The No Nonsense Parenting Guide to Baby Names* gives you the meanings, origins and variations of thousands of potential names for your baby.

Many people prefer to choose a name reflecting a particular national origin. If you pick an unusual name, be careful that it is not too hard to pronounce or spell, since this can be an additional burden when your child is growing up.

HONORING LOVED ONES

Very often parents name their children after loved ones. You give honor to a close friend or relative when you name your child after them. But be sure that the name is also one that you like for itself.

It is traditional in Jewish families to name a baby in memory of a deceased loved one, while Roman Catholics often follow the tradition of including the name of a saint as the child's first or middle name.

Some families follow the tradition of giving their first-born son the father's name, modified by Junior (or III or IV, etc., as one generation follows another). For whatever reason, the use of Jr. has become more infrequent in this country in recent years. Perhaps this is because some dislike being called "Junior," or perhaps it is because of the confusion that occasionally arises. Many couples solve this problem by giving their new son the father's first name but a different middle name. Thus the family's first and last names are preserved, but the child can be called by his middle name if desired, and his initials will be different from

2

his father's. Other parents solve this problem by giving the son a different nickname from the father. For example, if the father is named Edward and nicknamed "Ed," the son can also be named Edward, but nicknamed "Ted," while the grandson, also Edward, could be called "Ned." (By the fourth generation, the family presumably can go back to "Ed" without fear of confusion.)

INITIALS

Make sure that your child's initials do not spell anything silly, funny or rude. Remember that in the future, your child's initials will appear on luggage, briefcases, etc. For example, Catherine Olivia Worthing sounds like a perfectly lovely name, but the initials, C.O.W., are quite unacceptable for any human female. On a similar but less obvious note, would you want your son to go through life with the initials of the seemingly pleasant name, Stuart Allan Dunnington? Be careful.

POPULARITY

Fashions in names can vary. Mary, John, Jane and William will probably always be popular. But other names, such as Jennifer, Jason, Blake, and Jessica have had popularity cycles. You should consider whether you want your baby's name to be one of the "old standards," to follow a popularity trend, or to fall outside either of these categories and to be more unusual.

UNIQUENESS

Many parents want to give their child a name that is unique and that will be associated with their baby and no one else. If your surname is common, you might want to choose a more distinctive first name for your baby. But be sure that the distinctive or unusual name doesn't become a burden to your child because it is unpronounceable, hard to spell, or so unusual that it becomes a source of humor.

If your last name is complicated and often mispronounced, adding a difficult first name may put an unfair burden on your

3

child. While you have been coping with your family name for many years, it might be wise to try to remember your childhood feelings. Would a simpler name have been easier for you?

MIXING GENDERS

In a similar vein, be careful of mixing genders. Psychologists tell us that girls who are given boys' names survive undamaged, but that boys who are given girls' names may suffer embarrassment or even real psychological damage. While it may be perfectly fine, psychologically, to name your little girl Leigh, Jordan, Ashley, or Morgan, it may not be wise to name your son Beverly, Carroll, Clair, or Hilary.

MIDDLE NAMES

Middle names have increasingly become the norm in the United States. In England and throughout the British Commonwealth, two middle names are commonly used. In the United States, one middle name is common, and the use of an initial as a middle name is not infrequent. (S was the middle name of President Harry S Truman—not Samuel or Stuart, just S, and without the period.) Where both the first and last names are common, a middle name can add distinction and help in identification. And a child who dislikes his/her first name can choose to be called by the middle name.

Often the middle name is taken from the father's or mother's first name, or from the mother's maiden name.

SPELLING

Be careful of how you decide to spell your baby's name. A common name, unusually spelled, can cause as many problems as a name that is too unusual. Take care also that the spelling doesn't create pronunciation problems.

4

NICKNAMES

When you like a name, consider the nicknames that are associated with it. Even if you intend that your little girl will always be called Cynthia, be aware that children and others will call her Cindy. If you don't like Cindy, don't pick Cynthia. If you don't like Dick, avoid Richard. And so on.

RHYMING

This guideline is simple—make sure that your baby's first name and last name (or the nickname and last name) don't rhyme. The cuteness will soon become distasteful.

NUMBER OF SYLLABLES

Some people think it best to have an uneven number of syllables in the combination of first and last names. If your surname has two syllables, so the argument goes, you should try to select a first name with one or three syllables. Similarly, if your surname has one syllable, consider a two-syllable first name. We find this guideline interesting but not always helpful. Sometimes it simply doesn't apply. In each case, your ear must be the judge.

LAST LETTER, FIRST LETTER

A name may be difficult to pronounce when the last letter of the first name is the same as the first letter of the last name. For example, Anna Atkinson and Robert Trent are more difficult to pronounce clearly than Anne Atkinson and William Trent.

Which brings us to the most essential rule of all—

SAY IT!

We can't sufficiently stress the importance of this final guideline. Say it! The sound, rhythm and harmony of your baby's name

can only be determined by saying the name over and over again.

You should Say It! in several steps. First, say the first name you select over and over. Say it while climbing the stairs. Say it in the car. Say it to friends and family. Say it in the shower. Are you comfortable with the sound, the poetry, the "feeling" of the name? If you are, then you should go on to the next "Say It!" step.

Combine the first name with your surname. Repeat them over and over together. How do they sound? Do you like the rhythm, the harmony, the feel of the combination? As with the first name alone, it may take days of repetition before you can be sure that the name you have chosen sounds just right.

Finally, repeat the process with the middle name or names included. Take all the names together and say them to your friends, relatives and aloud to yourself. Also, repeat the name, using only the middle initial. How does it sound? How does it look? Finally, check the meaning of the initials.

A GIFT TO CHERISH

The finest gifts give joy to both giver and recipient. If you have thought carefully and selected well, your baby's name will give joy to both you and your child, and will be a gift cherished throughout a lifetime.

Girls' Names

Abbe, Abby, Abbey   Abbreviation of Abigail.

Abela   Latin origin meaning "beautiful." Other forms include Abella, Abelia.

Abigail   Hebrew or Arabic origin (Biblical) meaning "my father's joy" or "source of joy." Other forms include Abagail, Abbe, Abbey, Abbie, Abby, Gael, Gail, Gaile, Gale, Gayle.

Abra   Hebrew origin (Biblical), the feminine version of Abraham.

Acacia   Greek origin meaning "a thorny tree" or "immortality."

Ada   German or Old English origin meaning "prosperous" or "nobly born." Often an abbreviation for Adeline, Adelaide, etc.

Adamina   Scottish origin. The feminine version of Adam.

Adelaide   See Adeline.

Adeline   German origin meaning "nobly born." Other forms include Adaline, Adelaide, Adel, Adela, Adele, Adelina, Adelle.

Adele   See Adeline.

Adelphia Greek origin meaning "sisterly."

Adena, Adina Hebrew origin (Biblical) meaning "delicate" or "voluptuous."

Adrienne French version of the Greek or Latin name "Hadrian," meaning "rich." Other forms include Adrea, Adrean, Adria, Adrian, Adriana, Adriane, Adrianna, Adrianne, Adriene.

Agatha Greek origin meaning "kind" or "good."

Agnes Greek origin meaning "pure" or "chaste." Other forms include Aggie, Annice, Annis, Inez.

Aida Italian version of Ada. The name of the heroine in Verdi's opera of the same name.

Aileen See Eileen.

Aimee French origin for "beloved." Alternative spelling of Amy.

Alanna Irish Gaelic meaning "beautiful." Also the feminine version of Alan. Other forms include Alana, Alayna, Allana, Allena, Alyne.

Alberta Old German origin, the feminine version of Albert, meaning "brilliant and noble." Other forms include Albertina, Albertine.

Alda Old German meaning "old" or "rich." The feminine version of Aldo.

Aleeza Hebrew origin meaning "joyous." Other forms include Aleza, Aliza.

Aleine, Alene See Alina.

Alethea Greek origin meaning "truth." Other forms include Aleta, Aletha.

Alexandra Greek origin meaning "defender of mankind." Other forms include Alessia, Alexa, Alexandria, Alexandrina, Alexia, Alix, Lexa, Lexi, Lexie, Lexine, Sandra.

Alexis A popular form of Alexandra.

Alfreda Old English meaning "wise counsellor." The feminine version of Alfred.

Alice   Greek origin meaning "one who tells the truth." Also Old German meaning "noble one." Other forms include Alicia, Alisa, Alisha, Allice, Allys, Alycia, Alys.

Alina   Celtic origin meaning "fair or beautiful one." Other forms include Alyna, Aline, Aleine, Alene.

Alison   Diminutive form of Alice. Other forms include Allison, Allyson, Alyson.

Aliya, Aliyah   Hebrew meaning "to go up."

Aliza   Hebrew origin meaning "joyous."

Allegra   Latin origin meaning "cheerful" or "lively."

Alma   Latin origin meaning "fair" or "nurturing." Also Italian origin meaning "soul."

Almira   Arabic origin meaning "princess."

Althea   Greek origin meaning "healing." Diminutive is Thea.

Alvina   Old English origin meaning "noble friend." The feminine version of Alvin.

Amanda   Latin origin meaning "loveable one." Other forms include Manda, Mandi, Mandie, Mandy.

Amber   Arabic origin (later also French) meaning the color amber (a rich brownish-yellow). Also refers to the gemstone of that name.

Amelia   Old German origin (possibly also Latin) meaning "hardworking." Other forms include Amalea, Amalia, Amalie, Amaline, Ameline, Emily.

Amethyst   Greek origin meaning "wine color"; used as the name of the gemstone.

Amity   French origin meaning "friendship."

Amy   French origin meaning "beloved," a form of the verb "to love." Other forms include Aimee, Ame, Amey, Ami, Amie, Amii.

Anastasia   Greek origin meaning "resurrection." Other forms include Stacie, Stacy.

9

Andrea Greek origin meaning "womanly" and "strong." Feminine version of Andrew. Other forms include Andria, Andee, Andi, Andie, Andy.

Angela Latin origin meaning "angel." Could also be from the Greek meaning "messenger." Other forms include Angel, Angelina, Angelita, Angelique.

Angelica Latin origin meaning "angelic."

Anita Spanish origin, the familiar form of Ann.

Ann, Anne Hebrew origin, originally Hannah, meaning "graceful." Other forms include Ana, Anna, Ania, Anya, Annie.

Anna See Ann.

Annabel A combination of the name "Anne" and "bella" or "belle," meaning beautiful. The name means "beautiful Anne," or "beautiful graceful one." Other forms include Anabel, Anabelle, Annabela, Annabelle, Annabella.

Annette Diminutive form of Anne. Alternative form: Annetta.

Annamarie A combination of the names "Anna" and "Marie" or "Maria." Other forms include Annamaria, Annemaria, Annemarie, Annmarie, Annmaria, Ann-Maria, Ann-Marie, Anna-Maria, Anna-Marie.

Anthea Greek origin meaning "like a flower."

Antonia Latin origin meaning "of high price." Feminine of Anthony. Other forms include Anntoinetta, Anntoinette, Antoinette, Antoinetta, Toni, Tony.

Anya Spanish version of Anna.

April Latin origin meaning "opening."

Arabella Latin origin meaning "beautiful altar." Other forms include Ara, Arabelle, Belle, Bella.

Aretha Greek origin meaning "virtue."

Aria Italian origin meaning "melody" or "song."

Ariana Latin origin meaning "song."

Ariane French origin meaning "holy one." Other forms include Arianne, Ariadne.

Ariel   Hebrew origin meaning "lioness of God." Other forms include Ari, Ariela, Ariella, Arielle.

Arlene   Irish origin meaning "pledge." Other forms include Arleen, Arline, Arlen, Arlena, Arlyne.

Ashley   Old English origin having to do with the ash tree and meadows. Other forms include Ashlee, Ashely, Ashleigh.

Astrid   Old Norse origin meaning "divine beauty" and "strength."

Athena   Greek origin: the name of the goddess of wisdom.

Audrey   Old English origin meaning "strong" or "noble." Other forms include Audra, Audry.

Augusta   Latin origin meaning "majestic" or "sacred."

Aurora   Latin origin meaning "dawn."

Ava   Latin origin meaning "like a bird." A separate meaning is as a variant of Eva.

Aviva   Hebrew origin meaning "in the spring." Other forms include Avivah, Viva.

B

Bab, Babs, Babette, Babetta   See Barbara.

Bambi   Italian origin, the diminutive form of the word meaning "child."

Barbara   Greek origin meaning "foreigner" or "stranger." Other forms include Bab, Babs, Babetta, Babette, Barbie, Barbra, Bobbie, Bobbi.

Bathsheba   Hebrew origin (Biblical) meaning "daughter of an oath." Alternate form: Sheba.

Beatrice   Latin origin meaning "joy giver." Alternate form: Beatrix.

Belinda   Probably of Spanish origin meaning "beautiful." A form of Linda.

Bella   Italian origin meaning "beautiful." Other forms include Bell, Belle.

Belle   French version of Bella.

Benita   Latin origin meaning "blessed." Other forms include Benedicta, Benedetta, Benetta.

Bernadette   French origin meaning "brave." The feminine version of Bernard.

Bernice   Greek origin meaning "one who brings victory." Other forms include Berenice, Bernetta, Bernita.

Bertha   Old German origin meaning "shining."

Bessie, Bess   Usually considered a familiar form of Elizabeth. Alternate form: Bessy.

Beth   Hebrew origin meaning "home" or "house." Also a short form of Elizabeth.

Bette, Betty   See Elizabeth.

Beverly   Old English name for a place near a stream populated with beavers. Alternate form: Beverely.

Bianca   Italian origin meaning "white."

Blaire   Irish origin meaning "one who comes from the meadow or plain." Alternate form: Blair.

Blanche   Old French origin meaning "white."

Blythe   Old English origin meaning "full of joy."

Bobbie, Bobbi, Bobby   See Barbara.

Bonita   Spanish origin meaning "pretty."

Bonnie   Scottish origin meaning "good." Other forms include Bonny, Bunny.

Brandy   Dutch and English origin meaning a prized after-dinner drink. Other forms include Brande, Brandi, Brandee.

Brenda   Irish origin meaning "raven-haired."

Bridget   Irish origin meaning "strong one." Other forms include Brigette, Brigida, Brigit, Brigita, Brigitte, Brigid, Brigitta, Gitta.

Brook, Brooke   Old English origin meaning "one who dwells near a brook or stream."

12

C

Cadence   Latin origin meaning "having rhythm."

Caitlin   Irish form of Katherine or Kathleen.

Camelia   Unknown origin, the name of a fragrant flower.

Camilla, Camille   Latin origin referring to a helper at a cere-mony.

Candace   Greek origin meaning "iridescent white." Other forms include Candee, Candi, Candice, Candy, Candada, Candida.

Caprice   Italian origin meaning "suddenly changeable" or "whimsical."

Cara   Latin-Italian origin meaning "dear one."

Carina   Italian origin, a diminutive of Cara, meaning "dear little one."

Caresse   French origin meaning "beloved."

Carissa, Carita   Latin origin, a diminutive of Cara, meaning "dear little one."

Carla, Carlotta   Latin origin, alternate forms of Carolyn.

Carmen   Latin origin meaning "song." Other forms include Car-meina, Carmine, Carmita.

Carol   Old French origin meaning "joyous song" (as in a Christ-mas carol). Other forms include Carole, Carroll, Caroll, Karol, Karyl.

Caroline, Carolyn   Latin origin meaning "petite and wom-anly." Other forms include Carola, Carolina, Carrie, Carla, Carlotta, Caryl, Karla.

Carrie   See Caroline.

Cassandra   Greek origin meaning "helpmate."

Cassie, Casey   Diminutives of Cassandra.

Catherine   Greek origin meaning "pure" or "truthful." Other forms include Catharin, Catheryn, Caterina, Cathleen, Cathy, Katherine, Katheryn, Kathleen, Kathy.

13

Cecilia Latin origin meaning "blind." Other forms include Cele, Celia, Ceil, Cissy.

Ceil, Cele Abbreviated forms of Cecilia.

Celeste Latin origin meaning "from heaven."

Celia An abbreviated form of Cecilia.

Cerise French origin meaning "cherry."

Chantal French origin connoting "song." Other forms include Chantel, Chantelle.

Charity Latin origin meaning "love."

Charleen A familiar version of Caroline.

Charlotte French origin, a version of Carol. Other forms include Charlotta, Cheryl, Sharline, Sharlene, Sharyl.

Charmaine French origin, a version of Carmen.

Chelsea Old English place name meaning "a port."

Cher, Cherie French origin meaning "dear" or "loved."

Cherry Old French origin meaning the cherry fruit.

Cheryl See Charlotte.

Chloe Greek origin meaning "young green sprouts."

Christine Latin origin meaning "Christian."

Cindy See Cynthia.

Cissy See Cecilia.

Clair, Claire, Clara Latin origin meaning "bright" or "shiningly clear." Other forms include Clare, Clarabelle, Clarice, Clarissa.

Claude, Claudia Latin origin meaning "lame." Other forms include Claudelle, Claudette, Claudine.

Cleopatra, Cleo Greek origin meaning "of great fame."

Colette Greek origin meaning "victorious."

Colleen, Coleen Irish origin meaning "girl."

Constance Latin origin meaning "faithful" or "firm." Other forms include Connie, Constantine.

Consuelo Spanish origin meaning "consolation." Alternate form: Consuela.

Cora, Coretta Greek origin meaning "maiden."

Corey Irish origin meaning "coming from a hollow place."

Cornelia Latin origin meaning "horn."

Courtney English origin, the surname of a prominent family.

Crystal, Krystle Latin origin meaning "of great clarity."

Cybil, Cybill See Sibyl.

Cynthia Greek origin referring to the goddess of the moon. Other forms include Cindy, Cindie, Cynthie, Cynthy.

D

Dagmar Old German origin meaning "famous of the Danes."

Dahlia Name of a beautiful flower.

Daisy Name of a pretty flower, a symbol of the sun.

Dana Scandinavian origin meaning "one from Denmark" or from the Hebrew meaning "to judge."

Danielle, Daniela Hebrew origin meaning "to be judged by God," the feminine form of Daniel.

Daphne Greek origin meaning "laurel."

Dara Hebrew origin meaning "wisdom."

Darcy Irish origin meaning "dark." A surname often used as a first name. Alternate form: Darcey.

Darlene French origin, a diminutive form of "darling."

Davida, Davina Hebrew origin, the feminine form of David, meaning "beloved."

Dawn English meaning "the break of day."

Deborah Hebrew (Biblical) origin meaning "bee." Other forms include Deb, Debora, Debra, Debbie, Debby, Devora.

15

Deirdre Irish origin meaning "one who wanders."

Delia Greek origin meaning "easily seen."

Delicia, Delise Latin origin meaning "delight."

Delilah Hebrew origin (Biblical) meaning "gentle."

Denise French origin meaning a follower of Dionysus, the god of wine. The feminine form of Dennis. Other forms include Denyse, Deniece, Denyce.

Diana Latin origin meaning "divine" or "pure." Other forms include Diane, Dianne, Deanna, Dianna, Diahann, Dyan.

Dinah, Dina Hebrew origin meaning "judgment."

Dolores Spanish origin meaning "sorrows." Alternate form: Delores.

Dominique French origin meaning "of God." The feminine form of Dominic.

Donna Latin and Italian origin meaning "lady."

Dorcas, Dorcia Greek origin meaning "gazelle."

Doris Greek origin meaning "a woman from Doria."

Dorothy, Dorothea Greek origin meaning "a gift from God."

Drusilla Latin origin meaning "strong."

Dugalda Irish origin, the feminine form of Dugald or Dougal, meaning "dark stranger." Alternate form: Dougalda.

E

Edana Hebrew origin meaning "child of paradise."

Eden Hebrew origin signifying a flat place or plain.

Edith Old English origin meaning "rich gift." Other versions include Edythe, Edie, Eydie.

Edna Hebrew origin meaning "delight" or "reborn."

Eileen Irish origin, a variation of Helen, meaning "light." Alternate form: Aileen.

Elaine   French origin, a variation of Helen, meaning "light." Alternate form: Elayne.

Eleana   Variation of Helen, meaning "light."

Eleanor   French origin, a variation of Helen meaning "light." Other forms include Eleanora, Elinor, Elinore, Leonore, Ella, Nora.

Eliana, Elianna   Hebrew origin meaning "my answer from God."

Elizabeth   Hebrew origin meaning "God's oath." Other forms include Elisabeth, Eliza, Lisa, Liza, Beth, Bette, Betty, Isabel, Libby, Lisabeth, Lillybeth.

Ella   Old English origin meaning "beautiful maiden."

Ellen, Ellyn   An English variation of Helen, meaning "light."

Eloise, Eloisa   Latin or German origin, variations of Louise or Heloise.

Elsa   German origin meaning "swan."

Elsie   Scottish variation of Elizabeth.

Elspeth   Scottish variation of Elizabeth.

Emerald   French origin meaning "a brilliant green" (as in the gemstone of that color.)

Emily   Latin origin meaning "industrious." Other forms include Emmy, Emilie, Emilia. See Amelia.

Emma   Old German origin meaning "universal."

Erica, Erika   Scandinavian origin meaning "powerful." The feminine form of Eric.

Erin   Irish origin meaning "Ireland."

Erma   See Irma.

Ernestine, Ernesta   Old English origin, the feminine form of Ernest, meaning "earnest."

Estelle, Estella   Latin origin meaning "star." Alternate form: Stella.

Esther   Persian and Hebrew (Biblical) origin meaning "star."

Ethel   Old English, or possibly Old German, origin meaning "noble."

Eugenia Greek origin meaning "nobly born." The feminine form of Eugene.

Eunice Greek origin meaning "victorious."

Evangeline, Evangelina Greek origin meaning "the bringer of good tidings."

Eve, Eva Hebrew origin meaning "life." Other forms include Ava, Evita, Evie.

Evelyn, Evelina Irish origin meaning "light," a version of Helen.

F

Faith Latin origin meaning "trust."

Fallon Irish origin meaning "descendant of a ruler."

Fanny See Frances.

Farrah English origin meaning "beautiful."

Fay, Faye French origin meaning "elf." Also probably an abbreviation of Faith.

Felicia Latin origin meaning "happy."

Felicity Latin origin meaning "happy" or "lucky."

Fern Old English origin meaning a small plant.

Fidelity, Fidelia Latin origin meaning "faithful."

Fiona Irish origin meaning "fair."

Fleur, Fleurette French origin meaning "flower."

Flora Latin origin meaning "flower." Other forms include Florella, Florelle.

Florence Latin origin meaning "flowering." Other forms include Florance, Flo, Floria, Flossy.

Floretta An adaptation of Fleurette, meaning "little flower."

Frances Latin origin meaning "liberal" or "one from France." Other forms include Fran, Francy, Fanny, Francine, Franny, Frankie, Francyn.

Francesca   Italian origin, a diminutive of Frances.

Francoise   French origin, a variation of Frances.

Freda, Freida   Old German origin meaning "peaceful." Other forms include Freeda, Freada.

Frederica   Old German origin meaning "peaceful ruler." The feminine form of Frederic.

G

Gabrielle, Gabriella   Hebrew origin meaning "my strength is God." The feminine form of Gabriel. Other forms include Gabi, Gabriela, Gaby.

Gail, Gale   Old English origin, a short form of Abigail, meaning "source of joy." Other forms include Gaele (Welsh spelling), Gael, Gayle.

Gay, Gaye   French origin meaning "lively" or "happy."

Gemma   Italian origin meaning "gemstone."

Genevieve   Old German (and possibly French) origin meaning "white wave."

Georgeanne   Greek origin, a familiar form of Georgia. Other forms include Georgeanna, Georgette, Georgena, Georgina.

Georgia   Greek origin meaning "farmer." The feminine version of George.

Geraldine   Old German origin meaning "warrior." The feminine form of Gerald.

Geri, Gerry   Diminutive forms of Geraldine.

Germaine   French origin meaning "from Germany."

Gertrude   Old German origin meaning "female warrior" or "strong with a spear." Other forms include Gertie, Gertina, Gert, Gertruda, Gigi, Gigs, Trudy, Trudie, Trudi.

Gila   Hebrew origin meaning "joy." Other forms include Gilah, Gilia.

Gilda   Old English origin (Celtic) meaning "helper of God."

Gillian Latin origin meaning "youthful." Other forms include Gilli, Gillie, Jill, Jillie.

Gina Hebrew origin meaning "gardenplace." Also an abbreviation of Regina.

Ginger Latin origin connoting the ginger spice or its flower. Also a form of the name Virginia.

Gisa Old German origin meaning "gift." Alternate form: Giza.

Giselle Old German origin meaning "sword" or "pledge." Other forms include Gisela, Gisele.

Gita Yiddish origin meaning "good." Also spelled Gitah.

Gladys The Welsh version of Claudia, meaning "lame."

Glenda Welsh origin meaning "good and holy."

Gloria Latin origin meaning "glorious." Other forms include Glora, Glori, Glorianne.

Glynis Welsh origin meaning "small valley." Other forms include Glenna, Glynnis, Glyn.

Godiva Old English meaning "God's gift."

Golda, Goldie Old English origin meaning "hair of gold." Alternate form: Golden.

Grace Latin origin meaning "grace." Gracie is the familiar form.

Greer Feminine version of Gregory, meaning "vigilant."

Greta Greek origin meaning "pearl," a familiar form of Margaret. Other forms include Gretchen, Gretta.

Gretchen See Greta.

Guinevere Welsh origin meaning "white" or "fair."

Gussie, Gussella Familiar forms of Augusta, meaning "sacred."

Gwendolyn, Gweneth Welsh origin meaning "white" or "beautiful." Other forms include Gwen, Gwenith, Gwenlian, Gwenneth, Gwennie, Gwyn, Winnie.

Isadora   Greek origin meaning "gift of Isis." The feminine version of Isidore.

Isolda   Welsh origin meaning "fair." Other forms include Isolde, Yseult.

Ivana   Feminine version of Ivan, a Russian version of John.

Ivory, Iverine, Ivorina   The name of the substance used as a first name.

Ivy   The name of the plant used as a first name.

J

Jacinta   Greek origin meaning "hyacinth."

Jacoba   Hebrew origin meaning "protector." A feminine version of Jacob.

Jacqueline   Hebrew origin meaning "protector." A feminine version of Jacob. Other forms include Jackie, Jacky, Jacki, Jacquelin, Jacquelyn, Jaqueline, Jackelyn, Jaclin, Jaclyn.

Jade   Spanish origin referring to the stone and/or color. Alternate form: Jayde.

Jamie   Hebrew origin meaning "supplanter." A feminine version of James and Jacob. Other forms include Jami, Jayme, Jaymee.

Jan   Familiar form of Jane or Janet.

Jane   Hebrew origin meaning "gracious." The feminine version of John. Other forms include Jayne, Jaine, Jana, Jaynie, Janessa, Janis, Jen.

Janet, Janice, Janetta   Alternate forms of Jane.

Jardena   Hebrew origin meaning "descend." A version of Jordan.

Jasmine   Persian origin, pertaining to the flower and the plant.

Jean, Jeanne   Hebrew and French origin meaning "gracious." Other forms include Jeanette, Jeanetta, Jeanine, Gene, Jeannie.

Jemima Hebrew origin (Biblical) meaning "dove." Other forms include Jemmima, Jemmie, Jemmy, Mima, Mimma.

Jemina Hebrew origin meaning "right-handedness."

Jena, Jenna Arabic origin meaning "tiny bird."

Jennifer Hebrew origin meaning "graceful"; Welsh origin meaning "fair." Other forms include Jeni, Jenifer, Jennie, Jenny.

Jeri, Jerri, Jerry Familiar forms of Geraldine.

Jessica Hebrew origin meaning "the grace of God." Other forms include Jess, Jessie, Jessy, Jesselyn.

Jewel Old French origin meaning "gem" or "joy."

Jill, Jillian See Gillian.

Joan Hebrew origin meaning "gracious." Other forms include Joani, Joni, Joannie.

Joanna, Joanne Familiar forms of Joan. Other forms include Jo-Ann, Jo-Anne, Jo-Anna, Johanna.

Jocelyn Latin origin meaning "just." A feminine version of Justin.

Jodi, Jody Familiar forms of Judith. Other forms include Jodette, Jodie.

Joi French origin meaning "joy."

Jolie French origin meaning "pretty."

Jordan Hebrew origin meaning "descend."

Josephine Hebrew origin meaning "God increases." The feminine version of Joseph. Other forms include Josie, Josepha.

Joy, Joyce Latin origin meaning "joy."

Juanita Spanish origin, the feminine version of Juan or the familiar version of Jane or Joan.

Judith Hebrew origin meaning "praise." Other forms include Judy, Judi, Judie, Jody.

Judy See Judith.

Julia Greek or Latin origin meaning "soft of hair." Other forms include Julie, Juli.

Juliane, Juliana Versions of Julia.

Juliet, Juliette Diminutives of Julia.

June Latin origin meaning the month.

Justina, Justine Latin origin meaning "just." Feminine versions of Justin.

K

Kara A variation of Cara.

Karen, Karina Greek origin meaning "pure." Other forms include Caren, Carin, Karyn.

Kate, Katie, Katy Familiar forms of Katherine.

Katherine Greek origin meaning "pure." See Catherine.

Kathleen Variation of Catherine.

Kathy Familiar form of Katherine or Catherine.

Kay, Kaye Familiar form of Kate, Katherine, Kathleen, etc.

Kelly Irish origin meaning "warrior."

Kelsey English place name.

Keren Hebrew origin meaning "animal's horn."

Kerry, Keri Irish origin meaning "dark."

Kesia African origin meaning "favorite."

Kim Familiar form of Kimberly.

Kimberly Old English origin meaning "royal fortress meadow."

Kirsty Scottish origin, familiar form of Christine.

Kitty Familiar form of Kathleen or Katherine.

Kristen, Kristin Latin origin meaning "follower of Christ."

Krystle See Crystal. Other forms include Krystal, Kristal.

Kyla The feminine version of Kyle, of Irish/Scottish origin.

Kyra Greek origin meaning "lord."

L

Lacey, Lacie French surname used as first name.

Ladonna French origin meaning "the lady." Other forms include Ladonne, Ladonya.

Laila, Layla Hebrew origin meaning "of the night."

Lakeisha, Lakisha French and Arabic origin meaning "the woman."

Lalita Sanskrit origin meaning "guileless."

Lana, Lanna Abbreviated version of Helen or Alana.

Lane, Layne English origin meaning "small road."

Lanette English origin for "very small road."

Lani Hawaiian origin meaning "sky."

Lara Latin origin meaning "famous."

Laraine, Larraine Latin origin meaning "a bird of the sea" or "gull."

Larissa Latin origin meaning "with cheer."

Lark English origin from the bird of that name.

Laura, Lauren Latin origin meaning "laurel leaves" or "laurel tree." Other forms include Lara, Lari, Laurel, Lauryn, Laurette, Lorette, Loretta, Laureen, Laureena, Lorinda, Loren, Lorena, Lorrie, Lorry, Lora, Lori.

Laverne French origin meaning "from the green place."

Lavinia Latin origin meaning "one from Latin places." Other forms include Lavina, Levina, Lovina, Lovinia.

Leah, Lea Hebrew origin (Biblical) meaning "weary." Lee is another form.

Leandra Latin origin meaning "lioness." The feminine form of Leander.

Leanna, Leane Hebrew origin meaning "bind." Other forms include Leanne, Leeanne.

Lee   Familiar form of Leah.

Leigh   Old English origin meaning "meadow." Also a variation of Leah and Lee.

Leila   Hebrew and Arabic origin meaning "night."

Lelia   Old German meaning "faithful."

Lena   Familiar version of Helena.

Lenore   A form of Eleanor, in common use in Russia.

Leona, Leontine   Greek origin meaning "like a lion."

Leonore, Leora   Other forms of Eleanor.

Lesley, Leslie   Old English origin meaning "land of meadows."

Letitia   Latin origin meaning "joyous."

Levona   Hebrew origin meaning "incense."

Lian, Liana, Lianne   Familiar forms of Gillian and Juliana.

Libby   Familiar form of Elizabeth. Other forms include Libi, Libbi, Libey, Libbey, Libbie.

Liberty   The English word used as a first name.

Liesl   German familiar version of Elizabeth.

Lilac   Persian origin referring to the flower name.

Lillian, Lilith   Latin origin pertaining to the lily. Other forms include Lil, Lill, Lilia, Lilli, Lilly.

Lily   Latin origin pertaining to the lily.

Linda, Lynda   Spanish origin meaning "handsome" or "pretty." Other forms include Lin, Linn, Linnet, Linnette, Lynn, Lyn, Lynne.

Lindsay   Old English origin meaning "linden" (a tree). Other forms include Lindsey, Lyndsay, Lyndsey, Lyndsie, Lynsey.

Lisa, Liza   Familiar forms of Elizabeth. Other forms include Lizzie, Lizzy.

Lisabeth, Lisbeth   See Elizabeth.

Lois   Greek origin meaning "desirable." Also a form of Louise.

Lola   Familiar form of Dolores and/or Louise.

27

Lolita Spanish familiar form of Lola.

Lora See Laura.

Lorelei German origin meaning "song."

Loren See Lauren.

Loretta, Lorinda Familiar forms of Laura. Other forms include Lorretta, Lorette, Lorrette.

Lorna, Lorne Old English origin meaning "forsaken."

Lorraine French origin meaning "from the Province of Lorraine." Other forms include Lorrayne, Lorayne.

Lottie, Lotty Familiar form of Charlotte.

Louisa, Louise Old German origin meaning "famous battle-maid." Other forms include Lou, Luisa, Luise, Lulu, Louiza.

Love English word needing no definition.

Lucia Familiar form of Lucille.

Lucille, Lucy Latin origin meaning "light." Other forms include Lucina, Lucetta, Lucinda.

Luella Variation of Louise.

Lunetta Italian origin meaning "little moon."

Lydia Greek origin meaning "a girl from Lydia." Other forms include Lydie, Lidia.

Lyn, Lynn Variation of Linda. Other forms include Lin, Linn, Lynne, Lynette, Lynelle.

Lyra Greek origin meaning "lyre."

M

Mabel Latin origin meaning "beautiful one" or "loveable one." Other forms include Maybelle, Mabeline.

Madeleine Hebrew origin meaning "high place" or "one from Magdala." Other forms include Madaline, Madeline, Maddi, Maddy, Magda, Magdala, Magdalene, Magdalena.

Madge   Familiar version of Margaret.

Mae   See May.

Magdalena   See Madeleine.

Maggie   Familiar version of Margaret.

Magnolia   Latin origin from the flower name.

Mahala, Mahalia   Hebrew origin meaning "tenderness."

Maida   Old English origin meaning "maiden."

Maisie, Maizie   Scottish familiar version of Margery or Margaret. Other forms include Maisy, Maizy, Mazey.

Malinda, Melinda   Greek and Old English origin meaning "sweet."

Mallory   Old German origin meaning "counsellor to the army."

Malvina   Irish origin meaning "chief." The feminine version of Melvin.

Mamie, Mame   Familiar versions of Margaret or Mary.

Mandie, Mandy   Familiar version of Amanda.

Manuela   Feminine version of Manuel.

Mara   Hebrew origin meaning "bitter." A familiar form of Mary.

Marcella, Marcel   Latin origin meaning "brave."

Marcia, Marsha   Latin origin meaning "brave." Familiar forms include Marci, Marcie, Marcy.

Mardi   French origin meaning "Tuesday."

Margaret   Greek origin meaning "pearl." Other forms include Margret, Margareta, Margaretta, Margarota, Margie, Margot, Marjie, Meg, Megan, Margery, Marjorie, Margaux, Madge, Maggie, Peg, Peggy.

Margery, Marjorie, Marjory   English versions of Margaret.

Margo, Margot   French versions of Margaret.

Marguerite, Margurite   French versions of Margaret.

Maria   Latin version of Mary.

Marian, Marianne   Hebrew origin meaning "bitterness." Other forms include Maryanne, Marianna, Mariana.

Marie   French version of Mary.

Mariel   Familiar form of Mary, used in France and the Netherlands.

Mariette   Familiar version of Mary.

Marilyn   Version of Mary.

Marina   Latin origin meaning "of the sea."

Marinda   Familiar version of Mary.

Marion   French version of Mary.

Maris, Marissa   Latin origin meaning "star of the sea."

Marla   Version of Mary.

Marlene, Marlena   Versions of Magdalena or Madeleine. Other forms include Marleen, Marlin.

Marlo   A version of Mary.

Marni   Hebrew origin meaning "rejoice." Other forms include Marnie, Marnina.

Marsha   See Marcia.

Martha   Aramaic origin meaning "mistress." Other forms include Marta, Martita, Marti, Marty.

Martina   Latin origin, the feminine version of Martin pertaining to Mars, the god of war.

Marva   Hebrew origin, the name of a type of mint plant.

Mary   Greek and Hebrew origin (Biblical) meaning "bitterness." Other forms include Maryann, Marybeth, Maryellen, Marylou, Maryruth, etc.

Mathilda, Matilda   Old German origin meaning "maiden of valor." The queen of William the Conqueror.

Mattie, Mati, Matty   Familiar versions of Mathilda.

Maud, Maude   French abbreviation for Mathilda.

Maura   Irish version of Mary.

Maureen Irish diminutive of Mary.

Mauve Latin origin meaning "lilac color."

Mavis French origin meaning "thrush."

Maxine Latin origin meaning "famous."

May, Maya Latin origin meaning "great," or Old English origin from the month of that name. Other forms include Mae, Mai, Maye.

Meg Familiar version of Margaret.

Megan, Meghan Welsh version of Margaret.

Melanie Greek origin meaning "dark." Other forms include Melany, Mellie, Melina, Mel.

Melinda See Malinda.

Melba Greek origin meaning "slim" or "slender."

Melina Greek origin meaning "honey."

Melissa Greek origin meaning "bee." Other forms include Melessa, Mellessa, Melisa, Missie.

Melody Greek origin meaning "song."

Mercedes Spanish origin meaning "grace."

Mercy English word used as a first name.

Meredith Old Welsh origin meaning "protector of the sea."

Merle, Meryl French origin meaning "blackbird." Other forms include Merril, Merrill, Merlina.

Merry, Merri Hebrew origin meaning "rebellious" or English origin meaning "pleasant."

Mia Italian origin meaning "mine."

Michaela, Michala Feminine version of Michael.

Michelle Hebrew origin meaning "Who is like God?" Other forms include Michele, Michaelina, Michaeline, Mickie, Micky, Micki.

Mildred Old English origin meaning "gentle strength."

Millicent, Millie Old German origin meaning "strength."

Mimi   Familiar form of Mary or Miriam.

Mindy   Familiar form of Melinda or Mildred.

Minerva   The Roman goddess of wisdom.

Mira   See Myra and Miranda.

Mirabel   Latin origin meaning "wonderful."

Miranda   Latin origin meaning "one who is admired."

Miriam   Hebrew origin meaning "bitter."

Missy, Missie   Familiar form of Millicent or Melissa.

Mitzi   German version of Maria.

Modesty   Latin origin meaning "modest."

Moira   Irish version of Mary.

Molly, Mollie   Irish version of Mary.

Monica   Latin origin meaning "advisor." Other forms include Monika, Monique.

Morgan, Morgana   Welsh origin meaning "very bright."

Moria, Moriah   Hebrew origin meaning "one who teaches."

Muriel, Murielle   Middle English origin meaning "merry" or Irish origin meaning "bright from the sea."

Myra   Greek and Arabic origin meaning "myrrh."

Myrna   Irish origin meaning "gentle."

Myrtle   Persian origin meaning "shrub." Also Greek origin for the plant of the same name.

N

Nadia, Nada   Russian origin meaning "hope."

Nadine   French and English version of Nadia.

Nan   Familiar form of Ann.

Nancy   Hebrew origin meaning "grace." Other forms include Nana, Nance, Nancee, Nanci, Nancey, Nannie.

Nanette   Diminutive version of Nan.

Naomi, Nomi   Hebrew origin (Biblical) meaning "beautiful."

Nara   Japanese origin meaning "oak." Also Old English origin meaning "near."

Natalie   Latin origin meaning "child born on Christmas" or "birthday."

Natasha, Natacha   Russian version of Natalie.

Nell, Nella   Familiar forms of Helen, meaning "light."

Nerissa, Nerida   Greek origin meaning "nymph of the sea."

Nessie   Scottish version of Agnes (familiar form).

Neta, Netta, Netty   Welsh familiar versions of Agnes.

Nevada   Spanish origin meaning "snow white."

Nicole   Greek origin meaning "people's victory." Other forms include Nicolle, Nicolla, Nicolette, Nicolina, Nicki, Nicky, Nikki.

Nina, Ninette, Ninetta   Spanish origin meaning "little girl."

Nita   Diminutive of Anita.

Noel   French origin meaning "Christmas." Other forms include Noelle, Nowel, Noella.

Nola   Latin origin meaning "little bell."

Nona   Latin origin meaning "ninth."

Nora, Norah   Latin origin meaning "honor."

Noreen   Irish diminutive of Norma.

Norma   Latin origin meaning "model" or "ideal."

Nova   Latin origin meaning "new."

Noya   Hebrew origin meaning "beautiful."

Nyssa   Greek origin meaning "place to start."

O

Octavia   Latin origin meaning "eighth."

Odelia   German origin meaning "rich."

Odessa   Greek origin meaning "odyssey."

Odette, Odetta   Versions of Odelia.

Olena   Scandinavian version of Lena.

Olga   Russian origin meaning "holy."

Olive   Latin origin meaning "olive" or "olive tree." Other forms include Olivia, Olivette, Oliva.

Olympia   Greek origin meaning "heavenly."

Ona, Oona   Latin and Irish origin meaning "the one."

Opal   English name of a beautiful gemstone.

Ophelia   Greek origin meaning "serpent."

Ordelia   Latin origin meaning "sunrise."

Oriel, Oralie   Versions of Aurelia, Ariel.

P

Page, Paige   French or Old English origin meaning "assistant."

Palma   Latin origin meaning "palm."

Paloma   Spanish origin (of Latin derivation) meaning "dove."

Pamela   Greek origin meaning "all sweetness." Other forms include Pam, Pamella, Pammi, Pammie, Pammy.

Pansy, Pansey   French origin meaning "growing."

Paola   Spanish variation of Paula.

Pascale   French origin meaning "a girl born on Easter." The feminine version of Pascal.

Patience   English word used as a first name.

Patricia   Latin origin meaning "patrician." Other forms include Pat, Patrice, Patsy, Patti, Patty, Tricia, Trish, Trisha.

Paula   Latin origin meaning "small." Other forms include Paulina, Pauline, Paulette, Polly.

Pavla   Russian variation of Paula.

Peace   Latin origin meaning "peace."

Pearl   Latin origin meaning "pearl." Other forms include Pearla, Pearle, Pearline, Perla.

Peg, Peggy   Diminutives of Margaret.

Penelope   Greek origin meaning "bobbin" or "weaver." Other forms include Pen, Penny, Penney, Pennie, Penina, Pennina.

Peony   Latin origin meaning "healing god." Also a flower name.

Pepita   Spanish familiar form of Josephine.

Perfecta   Spanish origin meaning "perfect."

Perry, Perri   French origin meaning "one who lives by the pear tree."

Peta   Feminine version of Peter.

Petra, Petrice, Petrina   Feminine versions of Peter.

Petula   Latin origin meaning "saucy."

Petunia   American Indian origin meaning the flower of that name.

Phedra   Greek origin meaning "bright." Alternate form: Phaedra.

Philadelphia   Greek origin meaning "brotherly love."

Phillippa   Greek origin meaning "horse lover." Other forms include Felipa, Fillippa, Phil, Philipa, Phillips, Phillippe, Philippa, Phillie, Philly.

Philomena   Greek origin meaning "beloved." Other forms include Philomene, Philomela.

Phoebe   Greek origin meaning "bright."

Phyllis   Greek origin meaning "little green bough." Other forms include Filide, Philis, Phillis, Phil, Phyl, Phyliss, Phylliss, Phylisse.

Pia   Italian origin meaning "pious."

Pilar   Spanish origin meaning "pillar."

Piper   Old English origin meaning "one who plays the pipes."

Pippa   Diminutive version of Phillippa.

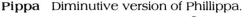

Pixie   English word used as a first name.

Polly   Latin origin meaning "petite." Also a familiar form of Mary, Molly, and Paula.

Pollyanna, Pollyann   A combination of Polly and Ann(a).

Pomona   Latin origin meaning "flourishing."

Poppy   Flower name of Latin origin.

Portia   Hebrew and Latin origin meaning "fruitful."

Precious   English word used as a name.

Primrose   English flower name.

Princess   English word used as a name.

Priscilla   Latin origin meaning "ancient." Other forms include Cella, Prescilla, Pris, Priscella, Prissey.

Prudence   Latin origin meaning "cautious" or "careful." Other forms include Pru, Prue, Prudi, Prudie, Prudy.

Q

Queen, Queena, Queenie   Old English word meaning "monarch."

Quentin, Quintin   Latin origin meaning "fifth." See Quinta.

Quinn   A variation of Queen. Also an Irish proper name.

Quinta   Latin origin meaning "fifth." Other forms include Quintina, Quintella, Quintilla, Quintana, Quentin, Quintin.

R

Rachel   Hebrew origin (Biblical) meaning "ewe." Other forms include Rachael, Rachele, Rachell, Rachelle.

Rae   Irish origin meaning "with grace." Also a familiar form of Rachel. Other forms include Ray, Raye.

Raelene   A version of Rae.

Raina   Russian version of Regina.

Raissa   French origin meaning "one who thinks."

Ramona   Spanish origin meaning "protector with wisdom." Also the female form of Raymond or Ramon. Alternate form: Ramonda.

Randall   Feminine form of Randolph or Randal, meaning "wolf counselor."

Randi   Diminutive of Randall. Other forms include Randee, Randy.

Raphaela   Hebrew origin meaning "God has healed." Alternate form: Rafaela.

Raquel   Spanish version of Rachel.

Raven   English word meaning the bird of that name.

Rayne   Yiddish origin meaning "pure."

Rea   Diminutive of Andrea.

Reba, Reva   Hebrew origin meaning "girl." Also a version of Rebecca.

Rebecca   Hebrew origin (Biblical), also Arabic, meaning "to tie." Other forms include Becky, Rebeca, Rebekah, Reveka, Rebbie, Reeba, Riva, Rivy.

Regan, Reagan   Latin origin meaning "queen."

Regina   Latin origin meaning "queen." Other forms include Regena, Reggi, Reggie, Gina.

Rena   Hebrew origin meaning "joy."

Renata   Latin origin meaning "born again."

Rene, Renee   Latin origin meaning "born again."

Rava   See Reba.

Rhea   Greek origin meaning "flower."

Rhoda   Greek origin meaning "rose flower."

Rhona   English version of Rona.

Rhonda   Place name of Welsh origin.

Riane   Feminine version of Ryan, meaning "red."

Richi, Rickie   Abbreviations of Frederica.

Risa   Latin origin meaning "laughter."

Rishona   Hebrew origin meaning "first."

Rita, Rheta   Sanskrit origin meaning "honest."

Roberta, Robertina   Feminine versions of Robert, meaning "famous wise one."

Robin   English word meaning the bird of that name. Other forms include Robyn, Robbi, Robby, Robina.

Rochelle   French version of the Latin word meaning "little rock." Other forms include Rochele, Rochella, Roshel.

Rolanda   Feminine version of Roland, meaning "famous throughout the land."

Rona, Roni   Hebrew origin meaning "joy."

Rosa   Latin origin meaning "rose."

Rosabel, Rosabelle   Latin origin meaning "beautiful rose."

Rosalie, Rosalia   French and Irish versions of Rose. Other forms include Rozalie, Rozele, Rosalee, Rosaleen.

Rosalind, Rosalinda   Spanish forms meaning "beautiful rose."

Rosalyn, Rosalin   American versions of Rosalind.

Rose   English version of Latin word meaning "rose flower."

Roseanne, Roseanna   Mixture of Rose and Ann(a). Other forms include Rosann, Rosanna.

Rosemary   Mixture of Rose and Mary. Also the name of a fragrant herb. Other forms include Rosemaria, Rose Marie, Rosemarie.

Rosetta   Italian familiar version of Rose.

Rosita   Spanish familiar version of Rose.

Rowena   Old English origin meaning "friend of great fame."

Roxanne, Roxane   Latin and Persian origin meaning "day-break." Other forms include Roxana, Roxanna, Roxi, Roxy, Rozanne.

Royce   Old German origin meaning "kind and famous."

Ruby   Old French origin meaning the ruby gemstone.

Ruth   Hebrew origin (Biblical) meaning "friend" or "compassionate." Other forms include Ruthy, Ruthie, Ruthe.

Ruthann, Ruthanne   Mixture of Ruth and Ann(e).

S

Sabina   Latin origin meaning "a woman from the Sabines."

Sable   Scandinavian origin meaning the animal of that name and its luxurious fur.

Sabra   Hebrew origin meaning "cactus." Name for native-born Israeli.

Sabrina   Familiar form of Sabra. Also Latin origin meaning "from the boundary."

Sadie   Diminutive form of Sarah.

Saffron   English word for the color and spice.

Sally   Diminutive form of Sarah. Other forms include Sallee, Salli, Salee, Sali, Sallyann(e).

Salome   Hebrew origin (Biblical) meaning "of peace."

Samantha   Aramaic origin meaning "listener." Other forms include Sam, Sami, Sammi, Sammie, Sammy.

Samara   Hebrew origin meaning "guardian."

Samijo   A mixture of Samantha and Josephine.

Samuela   Feminine version of Samuel, meaning "God heard."

Sandra, Sandy, Sandi   Familiar forms of Alexandra.

Sapphire   Greek origin meaning "precious blue gemstone." Other forms include Sapir, Sapira.

Sarah, Sara Hebrew origin meaning "princess." Other forms include Sarita, Sarina, Sarena.

Saran, Saranne A mixture of Sarah and Ann(e).

Sarina Adaptation of Sarah.

Sasha Russian diminutive version of Alexandra.

Scarlett Middle English origin meaning "scarlet color."

Selena, Selina Greek origin meaning "moon."

Selinda Mixture of Selena and Linda.

Selma Irish origin meaning "fair."

Serena Latin origin meaning "serene."

Shaina Yiddish origin meaning "beautiful."

Shana Female version of Shawn. Also, a variation of Shaina.

Shanell, Shanelle Alternative spelling of Chanel, the name of a famous clothing designer.

Shannon Irish origin meaning "wise." Other forms include Shauna, Shawna, Shanon, Shannah.

Shanta Familiar form of Chantal. Other forms include Shantalle, Shantele, Shantell.

Shari, Sharie Familiar form of Sharon.

Sharlene, Sharline, Sharyl See Charlotte.

Sharon Hebrew origin (Biblical) meaning "a type of rose" or "plain." Other forms include Sherri, Sherry, Sheirrie, Sharona, Sherye.

Sheba Adaptation of Biblical name Bathsheba meaning "daughter of an oath."

Sheena Irish and Scottish version of Jane.

Sheila Irish version of Cecilia. Other forms include Sheela, Sheilah, Sheelagh, Shela, Shelly.

Shelby Old English origin meaning "from the edge of the domain."

Shelley Old English origin meaning "meadow on the edge." Other forms include Shell, Shelly, Shelli, Shellie.

Sherry Latin origin meaning "queen" or French origin meaning "dearest." Other forms include Sheri, Sherri, Sherrie.

Sheryl Familiar form of Shirley.

Shirley Old English origin meaning "from the meadow that is white." Other forms include Shirl, Shirlee, Shirleen, Sherline, Shirline.

Shona, Shuna Irish feminine version of John.

Sibyl Greek origin meaning "a woman of wisdom." Other forms include Cybil, Cybill, Sibel, Sibella, Sybill, Sybille.

Silvana Hebrew origin referring to the months of May and June. Also the female version of Sylvan, meaning "woods" or "forest."

Simone Hebrew origin meaning "one who hears." The feminine version of Simon.

Sissy, Sissie Diminutive of Cecilia.

Sondra Abbreviation of Alexandra.

Sonia, Sonja Scandinavian and Russian versions of Sophia.

Sophia Greek origin meaning "one who is wise."

Sophie French version of Sophia.

Stacy, Stacie Abbreviated version of Anastasia. Other forms include Stacey, Staci.

Star The English word used as a name. Other forms include Starr, Starlene, Starletta.

Stella Latin origin meaning "star."

Stephanie Greek origin meaning "crown." Other forms include Stephana, Steffi, Steffie, Stephannie, Stephie.

Stevie Feminine version of Steve.

Storm, Stormy The English word used as a name.

Sue Abbreviated version of Susan.

Sunny English origin meaning "bright."

Susan Hebrew origin meaning "lily." Other forms include Susana, Susanna, Sue, Susi, Susie, Susy, Suzi, Suzie, Suzy, Suzanne, Suzan, Suzette.

Suzanne, Suzannah   Versions of Susan.

Suzette   French familiar form of Susan.

Sydney   Feminine version of Sidney, meaning "from St. Denis."

Sylvia   Latin origin meaning "of the forest." Other forms include Silva, Sylva, Silvie, Silvia.

T

Tabatha, Tabitha   Aramaic or Greek origin meaning "gazelle."

Talicia, Talisha   See Tabatha.

Talya, Talia   Hebrew origin meaning "heaven's dew."

Tallulah   American Indian origin meaning "jumping water."

Tamar, Tamara   Hebrew origin meaning "palm tree." Other forms include Tamarah, Tamera.

Tammy, Tami, Tammie   Abbreviation of Tamara. Also a feminine version of Thomas.

Tangerine   The English word used as a name.

Tanisha   Unknown origin.

Tanya, Tania   Greek origin meaning "sun."

Tara, Taryn   Irish origin meaning "pinnacle" or "hill" or French origin meaning "measurement."

Tasha   Familiar version of Natasha.

Temperance   English word used as a name.

Tempest   Old French origin meaning "storm."

Teresa, Theresa   Greek origin meaning "harvest." Other forms include Terese, Teresina, Teressa.

Terry   Abbreviation of Teresa. Other forms include Teri, Terri, Terrie.

Tess   Familiar form of Teresa. Other forms include Tessi, Tessie, Tessy.

Tessa Greek origin meaning "fourth."

Thalia Greek origin meaning "blooming."

Thea Greek goddess, an abbreviation of Althea or Dorothy.

Thelma Greek origin meaning "infant."

Theodora Feminine version form of Theodore, meaning, in Greek, "gift of God."

Theresa See Teresa.

Thomasa, Thomasin, Thomasina Feminine versions of Thomas, meaning "twin." Of Aramaic and Hebrew origin.

Tia Spanish origin meaning "aunt."

Tiberia Latin origin meaning "from the Tiber River."

Tiffany Greek origin meaning "divine appearance." Other forms include Tiffi, Tiffie, Tiffy, Tiphani.

Tila, Til, Tillie, Tilly Familiar forms of Matilda.

Tina Abbreviation of Christina.

Titania Greek origin meaning "huge" or "giant."

Toby Hebrew origin meaning "good." Other forms include Tobe, Tobey, Tobi, Tobye.

Toni, Tonia, Tonja, Tony Abbreviations of Antonia.

Topaz Latin origin meaning the gemstone of that name.

Tory, Tori Diminutive of Victoria.

Tourmaline English word for the gemstone of that name.

Tovah, Tova Hebrew origin meaning "good."

Tracy Irish origin meaning "brave" or Greek origin meaning "one from Thera." Other forms include Trace, Tracey, Traci, Tracie.

Tricia, Trish, Trisha Abbreviations of Patricia.

Trina Abbreviation of Catherine, Katrina, or Petrina.

Trista Latin origin meaning "sadness."

Trixie Diminutive of Beatrice.

Trudy, Trudi   Familiar form of Gertrude.

Tuesday   English day name.

Twyla, Twila   English origin of unknown meaning, possibly an abbreviation of "twilight."

Tyne   Old English origin meaning "stream" or "river."

U

Ultima   Latin origin meaning "distant one."

Una   Irish origin meaning "lamb" or "gift from the sea."

Undine   Latin origin meaning "water sprite."

Urice   Hebrew origin meaning "bright" or "light."

Ursula   Latin origin meaning "little female bear."

V

Valentina, Valentine   Latin origin meaning "healthy one."

Valerie   Latin origin meaning "strong." Other forms include Val, Valeria, Valery, Velery.

Vanessa, Vanetta   Greek origin meaning "butterfly."

Velma   A form of Wilhelmina.

Velvet   English word used as a name.

Venus   Latin origin meaning "beautiful." The goddess of love.

Vera   Russian origin meaning "faith" or Latin origin meaning "true."

Verena   Latin origin meaning "faith."

Verity   English word used as a name.

Verna, Verne   Latin origin meaning "like the spring."

Veronica   Latin origin meaning "truth."

Vicky, Vicki   Abbreviation of Victoria.

Victoria   Latin origin meaning "victorious." Other forms include Vicki, Vickie, Vicky, Viki, Vikki, Vikkie, Tori, Tory.

Vida, Veda   Abbreviation of Davida.

Viola, Violet   Latin origin meaning "violet flower."

Virginia   Latin origin meaning "pure."

Vivian   Latin origin meaning "alive." Other forms include Vivien, Vivienne, Viv, Vyvian, Vivyan.

W

Wallis   Scottish origin meaning "one from Wales."

Wanda, Wenda   Old German origin meaning "one who wanders."

Wendy   Abbreviation of Gwendolyn or Genevieve.

Whitney   English family name used as a first name.

Wilhelmina   Old German origin meaning "ruler."

Willa   Abbreviation of Wilhelmina. The feminine version of Wilhelm.

Willow   English name of a tree used as first name.

Wilma   Diminutive of Wilhelmina.

Winifred, Winnifred   Old German origin meaning "friend of peace."

Winnie, Winny   Abbreviations of Winifred.

Wren   English bird name.

Wynne, Wyn   Welsh origin meaning "white."

X

Xaviera   Arabic origin meaning "shining."

Xena Greek origin meaning "great."

Xenia Greek origin meaning "hospitable."

Y

Yedida, Yedidah Hebrew origin meaning "dear friend."

Yetta Abbreviation of Henrietta.

Yolanda Latin origin meaning "violet."

Yvette Diminutive form of Yvonne.

Yvonne French origin meaning "archer."

Z

Zandra Diminutive of Alexandra.

Zara Arabic origin meaning "dawn."

Zelda Old German origin meaning "maid of valor."

Zena A version of Xena or Xenia.

Zeta The Greek letter "Z."

Zoe Greek origin meaning "life."

Zola Family name used as a first name.

Zsa Zsa Hungarian version of "Susan."

Boys' Names

A

Aaron   Hebrew origin (Biblical) meaning "shining." Other forms include Aaran, Aran, Aron, Arron, Erin.

Abbott, Abbot   Hebrew origin meaning "father." Familiar forms include Abbe, Abbie, Abby.

Abe, Abie   Abbreviations of Abraham.

Abel   Hebrew origin (Biblical) meaning "breath." Sometimes spelled Able.

Abelard   Old German origin meaning "determined."

Abiel   Hebrew origin meaning "God is my father."

Abner   Hebrew origin meaning "father of light" or "candle of my father."

Abraham   Hebrew origin (Biblical) meaning "father of the multitude." Other forms include Abram, Avram, Avrom.

Abram   Hebrew origin, the original spelling of Abraham, meaning "the mighty one is my father."

Absalom   Hebrew origin (Biblical) meaning "my father is peace."

47

Ace   Latin origin meaning "together."

Adair   Scottish origin meaning "one who lives near the ford by the oak tree."

Adam   Hebrew origin (Biblical) meaning "earth" or "red earth."

Addison   Old English origin meaning "Adam's son."

Adlai   Hebrew origin meaning "my ornament."

Adolph, Adolf   Old German origin meaning "noble hero" or "noble helper."

Adolphus   See Adolph.

Adrian   Latin origin meaning "black" or "dark one."

Ahmad, Ahmed   Arabic origin meaning "greatly praised."

Al   Abbreviation of Alan, Albert, Alfred, etc.

Alain   French version of Alan.

Alan   Welsh origin meaning "harmony." Other forms include Allan, Al, Allen, Alen, Allyn.

Alaric   Old German origin meaning "ruler."

Alastair, Alasdair, Alistair   Greek origin meaning "avenger." A variation of Alexander.

Alban, Albin   Latin origin meaning "white."

Albert   Old German origin meaning "brilliant and noble."

Alden   Old English origin meaning "old friend."

Aldo, Aldous   Old German origin meaning "old" or "wise."

Aldrich   Old English origin meaning "wise ruler."

Aldwyn, Aldwin   Old English origin meaning "old protector."

Alec, Alex   Diminutives of Alexander.

Alexander   Greek origin meaning "man's protector." Other forms include Alessandro, Alexio, Alexis, Lex, Alexandr, Alexandre, Alec, Alex.

Alexis   See Alexander.

Alf   Diminutive of Alfred.

Alfred Old English origin meaning "wise counsellor." Other forms include Al, Alf, Alfie, Alfy, Fred.

Alfredo Spanish and Italian versions of Alfred.

Alger Old German origin meaning "noble warrior."

Algernon Old French origin meaning "one who has whiskers."

Ali Arabic origin meaning "highest."

Allan, Allen See Alan.

Alonso, Alonzo See Alphonse.

Aloysius Latin origin meaning "wise."

Alphonse, Alphonso Old German origin meaning "of a noble family." Other forms include Al, Alf, Alonso, Alonzo, Fonsie, Fonz, Fonzie.

Alton Old English origin meaning "village."

Alvin, Alvan Old German origin meaning "friend to all."

Ambrose Greek origin meaning "immortal."

Amos Hebrew origin (Biblical) meaning "troubled."

Anatol, Anatole Greek origin meaning "rising sun."

Anders Swedish version of Andrew.

Andre French version of Andrew.

Andrew Greek origin meaning "manly." Other forms include Andy, Drew.

Angel Greek and Latin origin meaning "angel."

Angelo Spanish and Italian version of Angel.

Angus Scottish origin meaning "unique strength."

Ansel Old German origin meaning "divine helmet."

Anthony Latin origin meaning "praiseworthy" or "priceless." Other forms include Anton, Antoine, Antonio, Antony, Tony.

Antoine French version of Anthony.

Anton German and Russian version of Anthony.

Antonio Italian version of Anthony.

Archer Old French origin meaning "archer" or "one who carries a bow."

Archibald Old German origin meaning "extremely bold." Other forms include Archie, Arch, Archy.

Ardon Hebrew origin meaning "bronze."

Argus Greek origin meaning "careful protector."

Argyle Scottish origin meaning "Irishman."

Ariel, Ari Hebrew origin meaning "lion of god."

Aries Greek origin meaning "ram." The zodiac sign.

Aristotle Greek origin meaning "the greatest."

Arlen, Arlin Irish origin meaning "pledge."

Arley Old English origin meaning "wood with eagles or rabbits."

Armand French version of Herman.

Armstrong Old English origin meaning "one with a strong arm."

Arne, Arn Old German origin meaning "eagle." Diminutives of Arnold.

Arnold Old German origin meaning "one who has the power of an eagle." Other forms include Arn, Arne, Arnie, Arny, Arnauld.

Arrow English word used as a name.

Artemus, Artemas Greek origin meaning "a present from Artemis" (Goddess of the Moon).

Arthur Welsh origin meaning "bear strength." Other forms include Art, Artie, Arty, Artur, Arturo.

Asa Hebrew origin meaning "healer."

Ascot Old English origin meaning "one who lives in the cottage toward the east."

Asher Hebrew origin meaning "fortunate."

Ashley Old English origin having to do with the ash tree and meadows.

Ashton Old English origin meaning "from the place of ash trees."

50

Aubrey   Old French origin meaning "elf king."

August, Augustus   Latin origin meaning "majestic" or "exalted."

Augustine   Latin origin meaning "one who belongs to Augustus."

Austin   English version of August.

Avery   Old English origin meaning "elf counsellor."

Avi   Hebrew origin meaning "father."

Avidor   Hebrew origin meaning "father guardian."

Avram, Avrom   Hebrew variations of Abram, Abraham.

Axel   Old German origin meaning "promoter of peace."

B

Bailey   Old French origin meaning "bailiff."

Baker   English word used as a name.

Baldwin   German origin meaning "bold in war."

Barclay   Old English origin meaning "one who comes from the meadow of birch trees."

Barlow   Old English origin meaning "one who comes from the bare hill."

Barnabas   Aramaic origin meaning "exhortation."

Barnaby   English version of Barnabas.

Barnard   Variation of Bernard.

Barnett   Old English origin meaning "strength." Also a version of Bernard.

Barney   Familiar form of Bernard.

Barns   English place name.

Barrett, Barret   Surname used as a first name. Could be of Old German origin meaning "having the strength of a bear."

Barry   Irish origin meaning "spear."

Bart   Diminutive of Bartholomew, Bartley, Barton.

Bartholomew   Aramaic origin (Biblical) meaning "son of Talmai (the hill)." Other forms include Bart, Barthel, Bartholomeo, Bartlet, Bartlett, Bartley.

Bartley   Irish version of Bartholomew.

Barton   Old English origin meaning "barley farm."

Baruch   Hebrew origin meaning "blessed."

Basil, Bazil   Latin origin meaning "kingly."

Baxter   Old English origin meaning "baker."

Bayard   Old English origin meaning "the reddish-haired one."

Beau, Bo   Old French origin meaning "handsome."

Bellamy   Latin origin meaning "beautiful friend."

Ben   Hebrew origin meaning "son." Used independently or as a diminutive of Benjamin.

Benedict   Latin origin meaning "blessed."

Bengt   Swedish origin meaning "blessed."

Benito   Spanish variation of Benedict.

Benjamin   Hebrew origin (Biblical) meaning "son of my right hand." Other forms include Ben, Benji, Benjie, Benjy, Bennie, Benny, Benn, Benjamen.

Bennett   English version of Benedict.

Benny   Diminutive of Benjamin.

Benson   English version of Hebrew origin meaning "Benjamin's son."

Bentley, Benton   Old English origin meaning "from the meadow where the grass is bent."

Berkeley, Berkley   See Barclay.

Bernard   Old German origin meaning "courage of a bear."

Bert, Bertie   Diminutives of Albert, Bertram, Burton, or Gilbert.

Bertol   Old German origin meaning "extremely intelligent."

Bertram   Old English origin meaning "bright one."

Berwyn Old English origin meaning "intelligent friend."

Beryl Greek origin meaning "stone of great value."

Bevan Welsh origin meaning "Evan's son."

Bill, Billy Diminutives of William.

Birch Old English origin meaning "birch tree."

Bjorn Scandinavian origin meaning "bear."

Blade Old English origin meaning "glory."

Blaine Irish origin meaning "slim."

Blair Irish origin meaning "one who comes from the meadow or plain."

Blake Old English origin meaning "to whiten" or "to bleach."

Bob, Bobbie, Bobby Diminutive versions of Robert.

Bogart Old French origin meaning "strong."

Boris Slavic origin meaning "warrior."

Boyce Old French origin meaning "from the woods."

Boyd Scottish origin meaning "of yellow hair."

Brad Diminutive of Bradley or Bradford.

Bradford Old English origin meaning "broad valley."

Bradley Old English origin meaning "broad meadow."

Brady Irish origin meaning "high spirits."

Bram Dutch version of Abram, Abraham.

Brandon Old English origin meaning "hill with the beacon light."

Brendan Irish origin meaning "small raven" or "sword." Other forms include Bren, Brenden, Brendon, Brennan.

Brent Old English origin meaning "high place."

Bret, Brett Irish origin meaning "one from Brittany," a Breton.

Brian Irish origin meaning "strong" or "of noble birth." Other forms include Brion, Bryan, Bryant, Bryon.

Brigham Old English origin meaning "town near a bridge."

Brock Old English origin meaning "badger."

Broderick Scandinavian origin meaning "brother" or Welsh origin meaning "Roderick's son."

Brook, Brooks Old English origin meaning "one who dwells near the water."

Bruce Scottish origin meaning "woods."

Bruno Old German origin meaning "brown" or "dark."

Bryan Variation of Brian.

Bryn Welsh origin meaning "hill."

Bud, Budd Welsh origin meaning "rich."

Burgess Old English origin meaning "freeman" or "citizen."

Burt Diminutive of Burton.

Burton Old English origin meaning "town on a hill." Other forms include Bert, Burt.

Byron Old French origin meaning "one who comes from the cottage."

C

Caesar Latin origin meaning "long-haired." Also meaning "emperor" through use as the title of the emperors of Rome. Other forms include Cesar, Cesario, Cesaro.

Cain Hebrew origin (Biblical) meaning "spear."

Caleb Hebrew origin (Biblical) meaning "dog" or "heart."

Calhoun Irish origin meaning "from the narrow place in the forest."

Calvin Latin origin meaning "bald."

Camden Scottish origin meaning "crooked valley."

Cameron Scottish origin meaning "crooked stream."

Campbell Scottish origin meaning "crooked mouth."

Carey, Cary Latin origin meaning "expensive" or "of great value."

Carl Old German origin meaning "man." Other forms include Carrol, Carroll, Caryl, Karl, Karol.

Carlo Italian version of Charles.

Carlos Spanish version of Charles.

Carlton, Carleton Old English origin meaning "from Carl's farm." Also alternative forms of Charlton.

Carmine, Carmen Latin origin meaning "song."

Carroll, Carrol A variation of Charles. See also Carl.

Carter Old English origin meaning "one who drives carts."

Carver Old English origin meaning "one who carves wood."

Cary See Carey.

Casey, Case Irish origin meaning "brave" or "of valor."

Casper Old German origin meaning "imperial." Other forms include Caspar, Cass, Cassie, Cassy.

Cass See Casper.

Cecil Latin origin meaning "blind."

Cedric Welsh origin meaning "plentiful."

Chad Old English origin meaning "warrior." Abbreviation of Chadwick.

Chadwick Old English origin meaning "warrior's town."

Chaim Hebrew origin meaning "life." Other forms include Hy, Hyman, Hymie.

Chandler Old French origin meaning "one who makes candles."

Charles Old German origin meaning "strong man." Other forms include Charlie, Charly, Carlo, Carlos, Chas, Chip, Chuck.

Charlton Old English origin meaning "town of farmers." Other forms include Carlton, Carleton.

Chauncey English origin meaning "churchman."

Chester Old English origin meaning "fortress."

Chet   Diminutive of Chester.

Chico   Spanish diminutive of Francis.

Chris   Abbreviation of Christopher, Christian.

Christian   Latin origin meaning "follower of Christ." Other forms include Chris, Christie, Christiano, Kit, Kris, Kristian.

Christopher   Greek origin meaning "bearer of Christ." Other forms include Chris, Christie, Christy, Christoph, Christophe, Kristo, Kristofer, Kristopher, Kristos.

Chuck   Variation of Charles.

Claiborne   See Clayborne.

Clancy   Irish origin meaning "kin of the red-haired warrior."

Clarence   Latin origin meaning "illustrious."

Clark, Clarke   Latin origin meaning "scholar."

Claud, Claude   Latin origin meaning "lame." Other forms include Claudell, Claudian, Claudius.

Clay   Old English origin meaning "clay from the earth."

Clayborne   Old English origin meaning "born of the earth." Alternate form: Claiborne.

Clayton   Old English origin meaning "of the earth," or "from the place built on the clay."

Clement   Latin origin meaning "merciful." Other forms include Clem, Clemens, Clemente.

Cleveland   Old English origin meaning "from the hills."

Cliff   Diminutive of Clifford.

Clifford   Old English origin meaning "crossing near the cliff."

Clifton   Old English origin meaning "village near the cliff."

Clint   Diminutive of Clinton.

Clinton   Old English origin meaning "town near a hill."

Clive   Old English origin meaning "cliff."

Clyde   Welsh origin meaning "heard from far away."

Colby   Old English origin meaning "one who comes from a charcoal farm."

Cole   Diminutive of Nicholas, Colby, and Coleman.

Coleman   Old English origin meaning "one who makes charcoal."

Colin   Scottish origin meaning "puppy." Also Irish origin, a diminutive of Nicholas. Other forms include Collin, Cullen, Cole.

Collins   Old English origin, a variation of Nicholas.

Conan   Irish origin meaning "king."

Conrad   Old German origin meaning "wise advisor."

Conroy   Irish origin meaning "wise one."

Constantine   Latin origin meaning "constant."

Conway   Irish origin meaning "from the holy Conway River."

Cooper   Old English origin meaning "one who makes barrels."

Corbet, Corbett   Latin origin meaning "black-haired."

Cordell   Latin origin meaning "cord."

Corey   Irish origin meaning "coming from a hollow place." Alternative form: Cory.

Cornelius   Latin origin meaning "horn" or "of horn-color."

Cornell   French version of Cornelius.

Cornwallis   Old English origin meaning "from Cornwall."

Cosmo   Greek origin meaning "universal harmony."

Courtney   Old French origin meaning "one who comes from the court."

Craig   Scottish origin meaning "crag."

Crawford   Scottish origin meaning "the stream where crows meet."

Creighton   Old English origin meaning "place of rocks."

Crispin   Latin origin meaning "curly."

Crosby   Scandinavian origin meaning "public cross."

Crosley   Old English origin meaning "cross-meadow."

Cullen   Irish origin meaning "handsome."

Culver   Old English origin meaning "dove."

Curt   Diminutive of Curtis.

Curtis   Old French origin meaning "courteous." Other forms include Curt, Curtiss, Kurt, Kurtis.

Cyril   Greek origin meaning "lord." Other forms include, Cy, Cyrill, Cyrille.

Cyrus   Persian origin meaning "sun."

D

Dale   Old English origin meaning "from the valley."

Dallas   Irish origin meaning "having wisdom."

Damien, Damian   See Damon.

Damon   Greek origin meaning "tame."

Dan   Familiar version of Daniel.

Dana   Scandinavian origin meaning "one from Denmark."

Dane   English variation of Dana.

Dani   Israeli origin meaning "my judge."

Daniel   Hebrew origin (Biblical) meaning "god is my judge." Other forms include Dan, Dannie, Danny.

Darian, Darien   See Darren and Darius.

Darius   Persian origin meaning "wealthy one."

Darnell   Old English origin meaning "hidden place."

Darrel, Darrell, Darryl   Old French origin meaning "dear one."

Darren   Irish origin meaning "great."

Dave, Davie   Diminutives of David.

David   Hebrew origin (Biblical) meaning "beloved." Other forms include Davon, Davy.

Davis   Old English origin meaning "David's son."

Dean   Latin origin meaning "schoolmaster." Other forms include Deane, Dene, Dino.

Dekel   Arabic origin meaning "date tree."

Del   Diminutive of names beginning with "Del."

Delano   Old French origin meaning "of the night."

Delbert   Old English origin meaning "bright day."

Delmer, Delmore   Old French origin meaning "from the sea."

Delroy   British version of Elroy.

Demetrius   Greek origin meaning "of the goddess of fertility, Demeter." Other forms include Dmitri, Dimitri, Demetre.

Dennis   Greek origin meaning "of the god Dionysus (the god of wine)." Other forms include Den, Denny, Denis, Denney, Dennison, Dion, Denys.

Dennison   A variation of Dennis.

Denny   Diminutive of Dennis, Dennison.

Denton   Old English origin meaning "valley town."

Denver   Old English origin meaning "crossing place" or "fertile valley."

Denys   French version of Dennis.

Derek, Derrick   Old German origin meaning "people's ruler." Other forms include Derk, Dirk, Derick, Dereck, Derrik, Theodoric.

Dermot   Irish origin meaning "free of envy."

Desmond   Irish origin meaning "one who is descended from someone who is from a place south of Munster." Other forms include Des, Desi, Desmund.

Devin, Devon   English place name.

Devir   Arabic origin meaning "sacred place."

Devlin   Irish origin meaning "brave."

Dewey   Welsh origin meaning "beloved." The Welsh version of David.

Dexter Latin origin meaning "right-handedness." Other forms include Dex, Deck.

Dick, Dickie, Dicky Diminutives of Richard.

Diego Spanish version of James.

Dillon, Dylan Irish origin meaning "faithful friend" or Welsh origin meaning "from the sea."

Dion Version of Dennis.

Dirk Dutch variation of Derek.

Dmitri Russian version of Demetrius.

Dominic Latin origin meaning "of God" or "belonging to God." Other forms include Dom, Domenico, Domenic, Domingo, Dominick, Nick, Nicky.

Don, Donny Abbreviation of Donald or Donovan.

Donald Scottish origin meaning "ruler of the world." Abbreviated form: Donny.

Donovan Irish origin meaning "dark hero."

Dorian Greek origin meaning "man from the city of Doris."

Doron Hebrew origin meaning "gift."

Dory Diminutive of Isidore.

Douglas Scottish origin meaning "dark waters." Other forms include Doug, Dougie, Douglass, Dougy.

Drew Diminutive of Andrew.

Duane Irish origin meaning "small and dark." Alternate form: Dwayne.

Dudley Old English origin meaning "meadow of the people."

Duff Irish origin meaning "dark face."

Dugald, Dougal Irish origin meaning "dark stranger."

Duke A title of nobility. Diminutive of Marmaduke.

Duncan Scottish origin meaning "brown hero."

Durand, Durant Latin origin meaning "enduring."

Durwood Persian origin meaning "guardian."

Dustin   Old German origin meaning "valiant warrior." Other forms include Dustie, Dusty.

Dwayne   See Duane.

Dwight   Variation of Dennis; Greek origin pertaining to the god Dionysus.

Dylan   See Dillon.

E

Earl, Earle   Old German origin meaning "wise" or Old English origin meaning "noble."

Ebenezer   Hebrew origin meaning "rock of help."

Ed, Eddie, Eddy   Abbreviations of Edward, Edgar, Edmund, etc.

Edgar   Old English origin meaning "prosperous warrior."

Edmund, Edmond   Old English origin meaning "wealthy protector."

Edsel   Old German origin meaning "wealthy."

Edward   Old English origin meaning "happy guardian of prosperity." Other forms include Ed, Eddie, Eddy, Edouard, Eduard, Eduardo, Edvard, Ned, Neddie, Neddy, Ted, Teddie, Teddy.

Edwin   Old English origin meaning "prosperous friend."

Efraim, Efram, Efrem   Hebrew origin meaning "fruitful."

Egan   Irish origin meaning "small fire."

Egbert   Old English origin meaning "shining sword."

Elazar   Hebrew origin meaning "the one God has helped."

Elden, Eldon, Elder   Old English origin meaning "older."

Eldred   Old English origin meaning "wise counsellor."

Eli, Ely   Hebrew origin (Biblical) meaning "rising up" or height."

Elias   Greek version of Elijah.

Eliezer   Hebrew origin (Biblical) meaning "my God has aided." Other forms include Elazar, Eleazar.

Elijah   Hebrew origin (Biblical) meaning "the Lord is my God."

Elisha   Hebrew origin (Biblical) meaning "God is my salvation."

Ellery   Latin origin meaning "of great cheer."

Elliot, Eliot, Elliott   Old English variation of Elijah.

Ellis   Variation of Elijah.

Elmer   Old English origin meaning "famous."

Elrad   Hebrew origin meaning "God is my ruler."

Elroy   A variation of Leroy.

Elton   Old English origin meaning "old village."

Elvis   Scandinavian origin meaning "great wisdom."

Elwin   Old English origin meaning "elf friend."

Elwood   Old English origin meaning "from the ancient woods."

Ely   See Eli.

Emanuel, Emmanuel   Hebrew origin (Biblical) meaning "God is with us." Other forms include Mannie, Manny, Manuel.

Emery   Old English origin meaning "conscientious ruler."

Emil, Emile   Old German origin meaning "conscientious."

Emmet, Emmett   Hebrew origin meaning "veracity" or "truth."

Engelbert   Old English origin meaning "angel bright."

Enoch   Hebrew origin (Biblical) meaning "dedicated."

Enos   Hebrew origin meaning "man."

Enrico   Italian version of Henry.

Ephraim   Hebrew origin (Biblical) meaning "fruitful."

Eric, Erik   Scandinavian origin meaning "powerful ruler." Other forms include Erich, Erick, Rick, Rickie, Ricky.

Erin   A version of Aaron.

Ernest, Earnest   Old English origin meaning "earnest." Other forms include Ern, Ernesto, Ernie, Erny.

Errol   Latin origin meaning "stranger."

Ervin, Erwin   See Irving.

Esau   Hebrew origin (Biblical) meaning "hairy."

Esmond   Old English origin meaning "protector with grace."

Ethan, Eythan   Hebrew origin (Biblical) meaning "strong."

Etienne   French version of Stephen.

Eugene   Greek origin meaning "nobly born" or "luckily born." Other forms include Eugen, Gene.

Evan   Welsh origin meaning "young warrior." Other forms include Evans, Evander, Evin.

Everett   Old English origin meaning "boar strength."

Ezekiel   Hebrew origin (Biblical) meaning "God will make strong."

Ezra   Hebrew origin (Biblical) meaning "help."

F

Fabian, Fabien   Latin origin meaning "one who farms beans."

Fairfax   Old English origin meaning "fair of hair."

Farley   Old English origin meaning "from the fair meadow."

Farnham   Old English origin meaning "meadow near river of ferns."

Farquhar   Irish origin meaning "most dear person."

Farrell   Irish origin meaning "hero."

Felix   Latin origin meaning "happy" or "prosperous."

Fenton   Old English origin meaning "town near a fen."

Ferdinand   Old German origin meaning "brave traveller."

Fergus   Irish origin meaning "strong choice."

Fernando   Spanish version of Ferdinand.

Fidel   Latin origin meaning "faithful."

Fielding Old English origin meaning "of the field."

Filmore, Fillmore Old English origin meaning "noteworthy one."

Finlay Irish origin meaning "hero with the fair hair."

Fisk Scandinavian origin meaning "fish."

Fitz Latin origin meaning "son." A nickname.

Fitzgerald Old English origin meaning "son of the mighty warrior."

Fitzroy Old French origin meaning "the king's son."

Flavio, Flavia Latin origin meaning "yellow hair."

Fleming Old English origin meaning "a man from Holland."

Fletcher Old French origin meaning "arrow maker."

Flint Old English origin meaning "creek" or "stream."

Florian Latin origin meaning "flowering."

Floyd English version of Lloyd. Also Welsh origin meaning "grey."

Forbes Scottish origin meaning "field."

Forrest, Forest Old French origin meaning "forest." Other forms include Forester, Foss, Foster.

Forster, Foster Latin origin meaning "one who works in the forest."

Francis Latin origin meaning "one who comes from France." Other forms include Fran, Francesco, Francisco, Frank, Frankie, Franky, Franz.

Francois French version of Francis.

Franco Italian and Spanish versions of Francis.

Frank Abbreviation of Francis, Franklin.

Franklin, Franklyn Old English origin meaning "landowner."

Franz German version of Francis.

Fraser, Frazer Old French origin meaning "strawberry."

Fred, Freddie, Freddy Diminutives of Frederick.

Frederic, Frederick Old German origin meaning "peaceful ruler." Other forms include Fred, Federico, Freddie, Freddy, Frederik, Fredric, Freidrich, Fritz.

Freeman Old English origin meaning "free man."

Fritz German version of Frederick.

G

Gabe, Gabie Abbreviations of Gabriel.

Gabriel Hebrew origin (Biblical) meaning "my strength is in God." Other forms include Gabe, Gabie, Gaby, Gabriello.

Galen Greek origin meaning "calm."

Gallagher Irish origin meaning "anxious to help."

Galvin Irish origin meaning "bright white."

Gareth, Garth Welsh origin meaning "gentle one."

Gardener Old German origin meaning "gardener." Other forms include Garden, Gardner.

Garfield Old English origin meaning "field of battle."

Garrett Old English pronunciation of Gerard. Other forms include Garret, Garreth, Garrot, Garrott.

Garrick Old English origin meaning "ruler with a spear."

Garth Scandinavian origin meaning "garden keeper." Also see Gareth.

Garvin Old English origin meaning "battle friend."

Gary Old German origin meaning "spear." Other forms include Garry, Garrie.

Gavin Welsh origin meaning "small hawk." Other forms include Gaven, Gavan, Gawen.

Gaylord Old French origin meaning "high-spirited lord."

Gene Diminutive of Eugene.

Geno Italian version of John.

Geoffrey Old German origin meaning "God's gift of peace." Other forms include Geof, Jeff, Jeffrey.

George Greek origin meaning "farmer." Other forms include Georg, Georges, Georgie, Georgy, Giorgio, Jorg, Yurik.

Gerald Old German origin meaning "spear warrior." Other forms include Gerard, Gerhart, Geraldo, Gerry, Gerri, Jerald, Jerrold, Jerry.

Gerard Old German origin meaning "brave with a spear."

Gershom, Gershon Hebrew origin (Biblical) meaning "stranger."

Gideon Hebrew origin (Biblical) meaning "to cut down."

Gilbert Old English origin meaning "shining pledge." Other forms include Bert, Bertie, Gilberto, Gilburt.

Giles, Gilles Greek origin meaning "one who carries a shield."

Gilroy Irish origin meaning "red-haired man's servant."

Gino Italian diminutive of Louis.

Giovanni Italian version of John.

Giuseppe Italian version of Joseph.

Glen, Glenn Irish origin meaning "valley" or "dale." Other forms include Glyn, Glynn.

Glenton Old English origin meaning "town in a valley."

Godfrey Old German origin meaning "peace of God."

Golding Old English origin meaning "of golden hair."

Goliath Hebrew origin (Biblical) meaning "stranger."

Gomer Hebrew origin (Biblical) meaning "famous in battle."

Gordon, Gorden Irish origin meaning "man of strength."

Graham Old English origin meaning "of the grey home."

Granger Old English origin meaning "one who farms."

Grant French origin meaning "to grant."

Granville, Grenville Old French origin meaning "from the big town."

Greg   Diminutive version of Gregory.

Gregor   Scottish version of Gregory.

Gregory   Greek origin meaning "vigilant man."

Griffith, Griffin   Welsh origin meaning "of powerful faith."

Grover   Old English origin meaning "of the grove."

Guido   European version of Guy.

Guillermo   Spanish version of William.

Gunther   Scandinavian origin meaning "warrior."

Gurion   Hebrew origin meaning "strong."

Gus   Diminutive of Gustav.

Gustav   Swedish origin meaning "war."

Guy   Old German origin meaning "soldier."

H

Hadar   Hebrew origin meaning "majestic."

Hadley   Old English origin meaning "from the meadow."

Hadrian   Greek origin meaning "wealthy."

Hal   Diminutive of Harold.

Haley   Old English origin meaning "healthy."

Hamilton   Old English origin meaning "from the big estate."

Hamlet   Scandinavian origin meaning "village."

Hanan   Hebrew origin meaning "gracious."

Hank   Diminutive version of Henry.

Hans, Hansel   Dutch, Scandinavian, and German versions of John.

Harcourt   Old French origin from a place name in Normandy.

Hardy   Old German origin meaning "hardy."

Harlan   Old German origin meaning "land owned by the army."

Harley Old German origin meaning "warrior."

Harmon Greek origin meaning "harmony."

Harold Old English origin meaning "powerful warrior." Other forms include Hal, Harald, Harry, Gerold.

Harper Old English origin meaning "one who plays the harp."

Harris, Harrison Old English origin meaning "the son of Harry."

Harry Old German origin meaning "mighty lord of the home." Also a form of Harold and of Henry.

Hartley Old English origin meaning "from the stag hill."

Harvey Irish or Breton origin meaning "able in battle."

Haskel, Haskell Hebrew origin meaning "wise."

Hastings Old English origin meaning "son of the severe one."

Hawthorn, Hawthorne Old English origin meaning "place of the hawthorns."

Hayden, Haydn, Hayes Old English origin meaning "from the valley of hedges."

Hayward Old English origin meaning "guardian."

Heath English origin meaning "heath" (a type of open land).

Hector Greek origin meaning "protector."

Hedley Old English origin meaning "place with heather."

Heinrich German version of Henry.

Henderson Old English origin meaning "son of Henry."

Henri French version of Henry.

Henrik Swedish version of Henry.

Henry Old German origin meaning "ruler of the home." Other forms include Hal, Hank, Harry, Hen, Hendrik, Enrico.

Herbert Old German origin meaning "excellent soldier." Other forms include Bert, Bertie, Berty, Herb, Herbie, Herby.

Hercules Greek origin meaning "gift of the goddess Hera." Name of Greek hero.

Herman Old German origin meaning "army man." Other forms include Armand, Armando, Harmon, Herm, Hermie.

68

Hernando   Spanish version of Ferdinand.

Herschel   Hebrew origin meaning "deer." Other forms include Hersch, Hersh, Hershel.

Hervey   See Harvey.

Hewitt   See Hugh.

Hilary, Hillary   Latin origin meaning "full of cheer."

Hillel   Hebrew origin meaning "highly praised."

Hiram, Hy   Hebrew origin (Biblical) meaning "born of nobility."

Hobart   See Hubert.

Holden   Old English origin meaning "from the hollow valley."

Holmes   Old English origin meaning "from the islands near the river."

Homer   Greek origin meaning "pledge."

Honi   Hebrew origin meaning "gracious."

Horace   Greek origin meaning "behold." Other forms include Horacio, Horatio.

Howard   Old English origin meaning "guardian."

Hubert   Old German origin meaning "shining mind."

Hugh   Old German origin meaning "intelligent mind."

Hugo   Latin version of Hugh.

Humbert   Old German origin meaning "giant Hun."

Humphrey   Old German origin meaning "intelligent Hun." Other forms include Humfrey, Onofredo.

Hunt   English origin meaning "hunt."

Hunter   Old English origin meaning "hunter."

Huntley   Old English origin meaning "meadow for hunters."

Hussein   Arabic origin meaning "small handsome one."

Hyman   Old German origin meaning "one who lives in a high place." Also of Hebrew origin meaning "life." Other forms include Hy, Hymie, Mannie, Manny.

69

I

Iago   Welsh version of James or Jacob.

Ian, Iain   Scottish version of John.

Icarus   Greek origin meaning "one who is a follower of the goddess of the moon."

Ichabod   Hebrew origin (Biblical) meaning "where is glory."

Ignatius, Ignace   Latin origin meaning "fiery."

Igor   Russian version of Inger.

Ike   Diminutive of Isaac.

Immanuel, Imanuel   See Emanuel.

Ingemar   Scandinavian origin meaning "notable son."

Inger   Scandinavian origin meaning "army of the son."

Ingram   Old German origin meaning "angel."

Ira   Hebrew origin meaning "watchful."

Irving   Irish origin meaning "handsome" or Old English origin meaning "friend from the sea." Other forms include Ervin, Erwin, Ernie, Erv, Irv, Irvin, Irwin.

Irwin   See Irving.

Isaac   Hebrew origin (Biblical) meaning "he who laughs." Other forms include Ike, Isaak, Isac, Itzak.

Isaiah   Hebrew origin (Biblical) meaning "my helper is God."

Ishmael   Hebrew origin (Biblical) meaning "God hears."

Isidore   Greek origin meaning "gift from the moon goddess Isis." Other forms include Dory, Isador, Isadore, Isidoro, Issy, Izzy.

Israel   Hebrew origin (Biblical) meaning "wrestled with God."

Ivan   Russian version of John.

Ives   Scandinavian origin meaning "small archer." See Yves.

Ivor   See Yves.

J

Jack Diminutive of John and Jacob. Other forms include Jackie, Jacky, Jock, Jocko.

Jackson Old English origin meaning "Jack's son."

Jacob Hebrew origin (Biblical) meaning "protector" or "supplanter."

Jacques French version of Jacob or James.

Jake Diminutive version of Jacob.

Jamal Arabic origin meaning "handsome." Other forms include Jamaal, Jammal, Jamil, Jamill.

James English version of Jacob. Other forms include Jaime, Jamey, Jamie, Jayme, Jim, Jimmie, Jimmy.

Jamie Scottish version of James.

Jan Dutch, Czech, Polish, Slavic versions of John.

Jared Hebrew origin (Biblical) meaning "descend." Other forms include Jarad, Jarred, Jarret, Jarrett, Jerad.

Jarvis, Jervis, Jary Old German origin meaning "excellent with a spear."

Jason Greek origin meaning "one who heals." Other forms include Jasen, Jase, Jayson.

Jasper Persian origin meaning "seeker of treasure." Could also be the English version of Casper.

Jay Old French origin meaning "chatterer" or "jay bird."

Jean French version of John.

Jed Arabic origin meaning "hand."

Jeff Diminutive of Jeffrey, Jefferson, Geoffrey.

Jefferson Old English origin meaning "Jeffrey's son."

Jeffrey See Geoffrey.

Jerald See Gerald.

71

Jeremiah Hebrew origin (Biblical) meaning "God will appoint" or "God will uplift."

Jeremy A variation of Jeremiah. Other forms include Jeramey, Jeramie, Jeremie, Jerry.

Jerold, Jerrold A variation of Jeremiah.

Jerome Latin origin meaning "sacred name." Other forms include Gerome, Gerrie, Gerry, Jerrome, Jerry.

Jerry Diminutive of Gerald, Jerome, Jeremiah, Jeremy.

Jesse, Jess, Jessie Hebrew origin meaning "wealthy."

Jethro Hebrew origin (Biblical) meaning "abundance."

Jim, Jimmie, Jimmy Diminutives of James.

Joab Hebrew origin meaning "my father is God."

Joachim, Joaquin Hebrew origin meaning "the Lord is judge."

Job Hebrew origin meaning "oppressed."

Jock Diminutive of Jacob.

Jody Hebrew origin meaning "addition."

Joe, Joey Diminutives of Joseph.

Joel Hebrew origin (Biblical) meaning "God is willing" or "Jehovah is God."

Johan, Johann Dutch and German versions of John.

John Hebrew origin (Biblical) meaning "God is gracious." Other forms include Giovanni, Hans, Janos, Johnnie, Johnny, Jon, Juan.

Jon Diminutive of Jonathan. Also alternate form of John.

Jonah, Jonas Hebrew origin (Biblical) meaning "dove."

Jonathan Hebrew origin (Biblical) meaning "God's gift."

Jordan Hebrew origin meaning "descend."

Jose Spanish version of Joseph.

Joseph Hebrew origin (Biblical) meaning "God increases." Other forms include Giuseppe, Jo, Joe, Joey, Jose, Jozef.

Josh Diminutive of Joshua.

Joshua Hebrew origin (Biblical) meaning "God is salvation." Other forms include Josh, Joshuah.

Josiah Hebrew origin (Biblical) meaning "God's fire."

Juan Spanish version of John.

Judah Hebrew origin (Biblical) meaning "praise." Other forms include Jude, Judas, Judd.

Jules French version of Julius.

Julian, Julius Latin origin meaning "soft of hair" or "downy beard." Other forms include Jule, Jules, Julie, Julio.

Justin Latin origin meaning "just." Other forms include Justen, Justinian, Justino, Justus.

K

Kalil Hebrew origin meaning "wreath." Also Arabic origin meaning "friend." Other forms include Kailil, Kahaleel, Kahill, Khalil.

Kane Welsh origin meaning "beautiful."

Kareem Arabic origin meaning "highly born."

Karel Dutch version of Charles.

Karl German version of Charles or Carl.

Kaufman German origin meaning "buyer."

Keane, Kean Old English origin meaning "keen."

Keenan Irish origin meaning "ancient and small."

Keir Irish origin meaning "swarthy skin."

Keith Scottish origin meaning "woods."

Kelly Irish origin meaning "brave fighter."

Kelvin Irish origin meaning "ship fancier."

Ken, Kenn Diminutive for Kenneth, Kent, Kennedy, Kenton, etc.

Kendall   Old English origin meaning "from the clear river valley."

Kennedy   Irish origin meaning "beautiful." Honors President John F. Kennedy.

Kenneth   Scottish origin meaning "handsome." Other forms include Ken, Kennie, Kennet, Kenny.

Kent   Old English origin meaning "border."

Kenton   Old English origin meaning "of the estate royal."

Kenyon   Irish origin meaning "of very fair hair."

Kermit   Irish origin meaning "man who is free."

Kerry, Keary   Irish origin meaning "dark hair."

Kerwin   Irish origin meaning "dark."

Kevin, Kevan   Irish origin meaning "handsome."

Khalil   Arabic origin meaning "friend." Alternate form: Kalil.

Kim   Diminutive of Kimball.

Kimball   Welsh origin meaning "royal chief."

Kingsley   Old English origin meaning "clearing in the woods of the king."

Kingston   Old English origin meaning "of the estate of the king."

Kirby   Old English origin meaning "church town."

Kirk   Scandinavian origin meaning "church."

Kit   Diminutive of Christopher, Christian.

Klaus   German diminutive of Nikolaus.

Knight   English word used as a name.

Konrad   A variation of Conrad.

Kris   Diminutive of Kristian or Kristofer.

Krishna   Hindu origin meaning "one who delights."

Kristian   See Christian.

Kristopher, Kristofer   See Christopher.

Kurt, Kurtis See Curtis. Kurt is also the German diminutive of Conrad.

Kyle Irish origin meaning "from the strait or narrow place."

L

Laban Hebrew (Biblical) origin meaning "white."

Lafayette French surname used as first name.

Lamar Old German origin meaning "famous in the land."

Lambert Old German origin meaning "famous through the land."

Lamont Scandinavian origin meaning "attorney."

Lance, Launce A variation of Lancelot.

Lancelot Old German origin meaning "land." Also Latin origin meaning "helper."

Lane English word used as a name.

Langdon Old English origin meaning "long hill."

Langston, Langsdon Old English origin meaning "from the long town."

Larry Diminutive of Lawrence.

Lars Swedish version of Lawrence.

Lavi Hebrew origin meaning "lion."

Lawrence, Laurence Latin origin meaning "one who wears a crown of laurel (a symbol of victory)." Other forms include Larrie, Larry, Laurent, Lauritz, Lonnie, Lonny, Lorant, Lorenz, Lorenzo, Lorin, Lorne, Lorrie, Lorry.

Lawrie Scottish version of Lawrence.

Lawton Old English origin meaning "hill town."

Layton, Leighton Old English origin meaning "from the farm with the meadow."

Lazar, Lazarus Greek version of Elazar.

Leander   Greek origin meaning "man with the strength of a lion."

Lee   Old English origin meaning "meadow."

Leif, Lief   Old German origin meaning "love."

Leighton   See Layton.

Leigh   A variation of Lee.

Leland   Old English origin meaning "from the land of meadows."

Lemuel   Hebrew origin (Biblical) meaning "devoted to God."

Len, Lennie, Lenny   Diminutives of Leonard.

Leo   Latin origin meaning "lion."

Leon   Greek origin meaning "lion."

Leonard   Old German origin meaning "lion strength." Other forms include Len, Lenard, Lennie, Lenny, Lennard, Leonardo, Leonid.

Leopold   Old German origin meaning "people's protector."

Leroy   Old French origin meaning "the king."

Les   Diminutive of Lester and Leslie.

Leshem   Hebrew origin meaning "stone of great value."

Leslie   Old English origin meaning "land of meadows."

Lester   Old English origin meaning "one from Leicester."

Lev   Hebrew origin meaning "heart." Also Russian version of Leo.

Levi, Levy   Hebrew origin (Biblical) meaning "to adhere" or "to attend to."

Lewis   See Louis.

Lief   See Leif.

Lincoln   Old German origin meaning "from the hill of the linden trees." Honors the sixteenth President of the United States, Abraham Lincoln.

Linden   Old German origin meaning "linden tree."

Lindsey   Old English origin meaning "linden (a tree)."

Linus   Greek origin meaning "blond hair."

Lionel, Lyonel   Old French origin meaning "baby lion."

Llewellyn   Welsh origin meaning "like a lion."

Lloyd, Loyde   Welsh or Irish origin meaning "grey."

Logan   Irish origin meaning "of the valley."

Lombard   Latin origin meaning "having a long beard."

Lon, Lonnie, Lonny   Diminutives of Alphonso.

Loren   Abbreviation of Lorenzo and Lawrence.

Lorenzo   Spanish and Italian version of Lawrence.

Lorn   Diminutive of Lawrence.

Lotan   Hebrew origin (Biblical) meaning "enveloper" or "protector."

Lothario   See Luther.

Lou, Lew   Diminutives of Louis, Lewis.

Louis   Old German origin meaning "warrior hero." Other forms include Lewis, Ludvig, Ludwig, Luigi, Luis.

Lowell, Lovell   Old English origin meaning "of love." Also Old French origin meaning "small wolf."

Lucas   Latin origin meaning "bright."

Lucian, Lucien   Latin origin meaning "light, shining."

Ludwig   German version of Louis.

Luigi   Italian version of Louis.

Luis   Spanish version of Louis.

Luke   Greek origin (Biblical) meaning "a man from Luciania."

Luther   Old German origin meaning "great warrior." Other forms include Lothario, Lutero.

Lyle   Scottish origin meaning "small."

Lyman   Old English origin meaning "a man from the valley."

Lyndon   Old English origin meaning "of the hill with the linden trees."

Lynn   Welsh origin meaning "lake."

M

Mac, Mack   Irish or Scottish origin meaning "son of."

Macdonald, McDonald   Scottish origin meaning "Donald's son."

Mackenzie, McKenzie   Irish origin meaning "ruler's son."

Madison   Old English origin meaning "great soldier's son."

Magnus   Latin origin meaning "great."

Mahommad, Mahmud   See Mohammed.

Mal   Diminutive of Malachi, Malcolm, Mallory, etc.

Malachi   Hebrew origin (Biblical) meaning "my servant" or "messenger."

Malcolm   Scottish origin meaning "disciple of St. Columba."

Mallory   Old German origin meaning "counsellor to the army."

Malvin   See Melvin.

Manfred   Old German origin meaning "peaceful man."

Manuel, Manny, Mannie   Abbreviations of Emmanuel.

Marc   French version of Mark.

Marcel   French variation of Mark meaning "small and martial."

Marco   Italian version of Mark.

Marcus   Variation of Mark.

Mario   Italian version of Mark.

Mark   Latin origin meaning "pertaining to the god Mars (god of war)" or "warlike" or "martial."

Marlon, Marlin   Old French origin meaning "small falcon."

Marshall   Old German origin meaning "keeper of the horses."

Martin   Latin origin meaning "pertaining to the god Mars (god of war)." Other forms include Mart, Marten, Martie, Martino, Marty, Martyn.

Marty   Diminutive of Martin.

Marvin   Irish origin meaning "rich mountains."

Mason   Old French and Old German origin meaning "one who works in stone."

Matt, Mattie, Matty   Diminutives of Matthew.

Matthew   Hebrew origin (Biblical) meaning "God's gift." Other forms include Matteo, Matthiew, Matthieu, Mathian, Matthias.

Matthias   Greek and Latin version of Matthew.

Maurice   Latin origin meaning "of dark skin."

Maury, Morey   Diminutives of Maurice.

Max   Diminutive of Maximilian and Maxwell.

Maximilian   Latin origin meaning "famous." Other forms include Max, Maxie, Maxim.

Maxwell   English version of Maximilian.

Mayer   See Meir. Other forms include Meyer, Myer.

Maynard   Old German origin meaning "strong."

Meir   Hebrew origin meaning "shining one."

Melvin, Melvyn, Malvin   Irish origin meaning "great chief."

Menachem   Hebrew origin meaning "one who comforts."

Mendel   Latin origin meaning "of great wisdom."

Meredith   Welsh origin meaning "protector of the sea."

Merle   See Merrill.

Merlin   Middle English origin meaning "hawk."

Merrick   English version of Maurice.

Merrill   Old German origin (and Old French) meaning "of great fame." Other forms include Merill, Merle, Merrell, Meryl.

Mervin, Mervyn   See Marvin.

Meyer, Myer   See Meir.

Micah   Hebrew origin (Biblical), diminutive of Michael.

Michael   Hebrew origin (Biblical) meaning "who is like God?" Other forms include Michal, Michail, Michel, Micheal, Mick, Mickey, Micky, Miguel, Mike, Micah, Misha, Mitch, Mitchel, Mitchell.

Miguel   Spanish version of Michael.

Mike   Diminutive of Michael.

Miles, Myles   Latin and Greek origin meaning "warrior."

Milo   German version of Miles.

Milton   Old English origin meaning "from the town with the mill." Other forms include Milt, Miltie, Milty.

Misha, Mischa, Mishka   Russian diminutives of Michael.

Mitch   Diminutive of Mitchell.

Mitchell, Mitchel   English version of Michael.

Moe   Diminutive of Moses or Murray.

Mohammed, Muhammad   Arabic origin meaning "greatly praised." Other forms include Mohamad, Mohamed, Mahommad, Mahmud.

Monroe, Munro   Irish origin meaning "marsh that is red."

Montague   French origin meaning "from the peaked mountain."

Montgomery   English version of Montague.

Monty   Diminutive of Montague and Montgomery.

Mordecai   Persian origin meaning "warrior."

Morey   Diminutive of Maurice and Morris.

Morgan   Welsh origin meaning "very bright."

Morley   Old English origin meaning "clearing in the moor."

Morris   English version of Maurice.

Mort   Diminutive of Mordecai, Morton, Mortimer.

Mortimer   Old French origin meaning "water that is still."

Morton   Old English origin meaning "from the village on the moor."

Moses   Hebrew origin (Biblical) meaning "delivered." Other forms include Moe, Moishe, Mose, Moshe, Moss.

Mosha   Hebrew origin meaning "deliverance."

Moss   Diminutive of Moses.

Muhammad   See Mohammed.

Murray, Murry   Irish origin meaning "man of the sea."

Myles   See Miles.

Myron   Greek origin meaning "pleasant odor."

N

Nadiv   Hebrew origin meaning "noble prince."

Nahir   Arabic origin meaning "shining."

Nahum   Hebrew origin meaning "consoled."

Napoleon   Greek origin meaning "lion from Naples."

Napthali   Hebrew origin (Biblical) meaning "wrestle." Other forms include Naftali, Naftalie.

Nat, Nate   Diminutives of Nathan and Nathaniel.

Nathan   Hebrew origin (Biblical) meaning "He gave."

Nathaniel   Hebrew origin (Biblical) meaning "God's gift."

Ned   Diminutive of Edmund, Edmond, Edward.

Nehemiah   Hebrew origin (Biblical) meaning "comfort of God."

Neil, Neal   Irish origin meaning "champion." Other forms include Neale, Nels, Niel, Niles, Nils.

Nels   Scandinavian version of Neil and Nelson.

Nelson   English origin meaning "Neil's son."

Nero Latin origin meaning "strict."

Neville, Nevil Old French origin meaning "of the new town."

Newton Old English origin meaning "of the new town."

Nicholas, Nicolas Greek origin meaning "victory." Other forms include Cole, Klaus, Niccolo, Nichols, Nick, Nicky, Nicodemus, Niki, Nikita, Nikoli, Nikolas, Nikolaus, Nikos.

Nick Diminutive of Nicholas or Dominic.

Niels Danish version of Neil, Nelson.

Nigel Latin version of Neil. Could also mean "black or dark brown."

Niles, Nils See Neil.

Noah Hebrew origin (Biblical) meaning "rest" or "peace."

Noam Hebrew origin meaning "friendship."

Noble Latin origin meaning "one of noble birth."

Noel French origin meaning "Christmas" or "born on Christmas day."

Nolan, Noland Irish origin meaning "famous."

Norbert Old German origin meaning "shining hero."

Norman Old English origin meaning "man who comes from the North." Other forms include Norm, Norbie, Normie, Normy.

Norris Alternate form of Norman.

Norton Old English origin meaning "from the North."

O

Obadiah Hebrew origin (Biblical) meaning "God's servant."

Octavius, Octavian Latin origin meaning "eighth."

Odell Old English origin meaning "from the hill with the forest."

Ogden, Ogdon Old English origin meaning "valley of oaks."

Olaf Scandinavian origin meaning "ancestor." Other forms include Olav, Olave.

Oliver   Latin origin meaning "peaceful man." Other forms include Olivero, Olivier, Oliviero, Ollie, Olly.

Ollie   Diminutive of Oliver.

Omar   Hebrew origin (Biblical) meaning "great speaker."

Oran   Hebrew origin meaning "tree." Other forms include Oren, Orin, Orren.

Orland, Orlando   Italian version of Roland.

Orson   Latin origin meaning "bear."

Orville   French origin meaning "of the town of gods."

Osborn, Osborne   Old English origin meaning "bear god."

Oscar   Old English origin meaning "spear of god." Other forms include Oskar, Ossie, Ozzie, Ozzy.

Osgood   Old English origin meaning "divine goodness."

Osmond, Osmund   Old English origin meaning "defender of God."

Oswald   Welsh or Old English origin meaning "power of God."

Otis   Old English origin meaning "Otto's son."

Otto   Old German origin meaning "wealthy."

Owen   Greek and Latin origin meaning "nobly born."

Ozzie, Ozzy   See Oscar.

P

Pablo   Spanish version of Paul.

Paddy   Diminutive of Patrick.

Palmer   Old English origin meaning "one who carries a palm."

Paolo   Italian version of Paul.

Paris   City name used as first name.

Parker, Park   English origin meaning "one who keeps the park."

Pascal   French origin meaning "pertaining to Easter or Passover." Other forms include Pascale, Pasquale.

Pat   Diminutive of Patrick.

Patrick   Latin origin meaning "patrician" or "noble person." Other forms include Paddie, Paddy, Padriac, Pat, Patricio, Patrizio.

Patton, Patten   Old English origin meaning "from the domain of the warrior."

Paul   Latin origin meaning "small." Other forms include Pablo, Paolo, Paulie, Paulo, Pavel, Poul.

Pavel   See Paul.

Paxton   Latin origin meaning "man from the town of peace."

Pedro   Spanish version of Peter.

Percival, Perceval   Old French origin meaning "one who attacks through the valley."

Percy, Percey   Diminutives of Percival.

Perry, Parry   Middle English origin meaning "man who lives by the pear tree."

Peter   Greek origin (Biblical) meaning "rock." Other forms include Pedro, Pete, Petey, Pearce, Peder, Peterus, Pierre, Peirs, Piet, Pietro, Peotr.

Peyton   Old English origin meaning "of the combatant's domain."

Phil   Diminutive of Philip.

Philip   Greek origin (Biblical) meaning "horse lover." Other forms include Felip, Felippo, Phelps, Phillip, Phillippe.

Phineas, Pincus   Egyptian origin meaning "dark skinned." Alternate form: Phinneas.

Pierce   English version of Peter.

Pierre   French version of Peter.

Pincus   See Phineas.

Porter   Latin origin meaning "keeper of the gate."

Preston   Old English origin meaning "village of the priest."

Q

Quentin   Latin origin meaning "fifth." Other forms include Quent, Quint, Quintin, Quinton.

Quincy   Old French origin meaning "town of Quintin."

Quinn   Irish origin meaning "strong." Other forms include Quin, Quinlan, Quinlon.

R

Radcliffe   Old English origin meaning "from the town near the red cliff."

Rafe   Diminutive of Rafferty. Also alternate form of Ralph.

Rafferty   Irish origin meaning "wealthy."

Rainer, Rainier   Alternate versions of Rayner.

Raleigh   Old English origin meaning "from the meadow full of deer."

Ralph   Old German or Scandinavian origin meaning "wise wolf counsellor." Other forms include Rafe, Rafer, Raff, Raoul, Raul, Rolph.

Ralston   Scandinavian origin meaning "village."

Ramon   Spanish version of Raymond.

Ramond   Variation of Raymond.

Ramsay   Old English origin meaning "from the island of rams." Other forms include Ramsey, Ramsden.

Randal, Randall   Variation of Randolph.

Randolph   Old English origin meaning "wolf counsellor" or "shield of a wolf." Other forms include Rand, Randal, Randolf, Randie, Randy.

Randy   Diminutive of Randolph.

Ransom, Ransome   English variation of Randolph.

Raoul   French version of Ralph and Rudolph.

Raul   Spanish version of Ralph.

Raphael   Hebrew origin (Biblical) meaning "God heals." Other forms include Rafael, Rafel, Rafaello, Rafe, Ray.

Ravi   Hindu origin meaning "sun."

Ravid   Hebrew origin meaning "ornamentation."

Ray   Diminutive of Raymond, Rafael, Raleigh, etc.

Raymond   Old German origin meaning "peaceful." Other forms include Ramon, Ray, Raymound, Redmond.

Raynor, Rayner   Old German origin meaning "mighty warrior." Alternate forms: Rainer, Rainier.

Redford   Old English origin meaning "from the crossing of the red river."

Redmond   Irish version of Raymond.

Reed, Reid   Old English origin meaning "red hair."

Regan, Reagan   Irish origin meaning "ancestor of the small king."

Reg, Reggie   Diminutives of Reginald.

Reginald   Old English origin meaning "powerful ruler." Other forms include Reg, Reggie, Reggy, Reinald, Reinhold, Reynold, Reynolds, Rinaldo.

Remington   Old English surname used as first name.

Rene   French origin meaning "born again."

Reuben, Rubin, Ruben   Hebrew origin (Biblical) meaning "behold—here is my son."

Rex   Latin origin meaning "king."

Reynard, Renard   Old German origin meaning "mighty warrior."

Reynold   English and French version of Reginald.

Rhett   Alternate form of Rhys.

Rhys Welsh origin meaning "ardour." Other forms include Reece, Reese, Rice, Rhett.

Ricardo, Riccardo Spanish version of Richard.

Rich, Richie Diminutives of Richard.

Richard Old German origin meaning "mighty ruler." Other forms include Dick, Dickie, Dicky, Rich, Richie, Rickie, Ricky, Ritchei.

Richmond Old French origin meaning "verdant hill."

Rick, Rickie, Ricky Diminutives of Richard, also of Eric.

Riley Irish origin meaning "brave."

Ring, Ringo English word meaning "ring."

Rip Diminutive of Ripley.

Ripley Old English origin meaning "from the place that shouts."

Roarke Irish origin meaning "great ruler."

Rob, Robbie, Robby Diminutives of Robert.

Robert Old German origin meaning "famous wise one." Other forms include Bob, Bobbie, Bobby, Rob, Robbie, Robby, Roberto, Roberts, Rupert, Ruperto.

Robin Diminutive of Robert or Robinson.

Robinson, Robson English origin meaning "Robert's son."

Rock, Rocky Old English origin meaning "rock."

Rod Diminutive of Roderick, Rodger, Rodney, etc.

Roderick, Roderic, Roderigo Old German origin meaning "ruler of great fame."

Rodney Old German origin meaning "of great fame."

Roger Old German origin meaning "man who is great with a sword." Other forms include Rodge, Rodger, Rogerio, Rogers, Ruggiero.

Roland Old German origin meaning "famous throughout the land." Other forms include Orland, Orlando, Rolly, Rollie.

Rolf, Rolfe   Scandinavian version of Rudolph.

Rollie, Rolly   Diminutives of Roland.

Romeo   Italian origin meaning "visitor to Rome."

Ron   Diminutive of Ronald.

Ronald   Old English and Scottish version of Reginald.

Roosevelt   Old Dutch origin meaning "from the field of roses." Honors Franklin D. Roosevelt and Theodore Roosevelt, Presidents of the United States.

Rory   Irish diminutive of Roderick.

Roscoe   Scandinavian origin meaning "from the forest of deer."

Ross   French origin meaning "red."

Roy   Old French origin meaning "king."

Royce   Old English origin meaning "famous."

Ruby   Diminutive of Reuben. Also French origin meaning "red stone."

Rudolph   Variation of Ralph or Randolph. Other forms include Rodolfo, Rusolf, Rollo, Rolfe, Rudolfo, Rudy.

Rudy   Diminutive of Rudolph, Rudyard, etc.

Rudyard   Old English origin meaning "red yard."

Rufus   Latin origin meaning "with hair of red."

Rupert   German, Italian and Spanish versions of Robert.

Russ   Diminutive of Russel.

Russel, Russell   Old French origin meaning "hair of red."

Rusty, Rustie   Diminutive of Russel.

Rutherford   Old English origin meaning "one who comes from the place where the cattle cross."

Ruvane   Hebrew version of Reuben.

Ryan   Irish origin meaning "red." Alternate form: Rian.

S

Sacha   See Sasha.

Salim   Arabic origin meaning "peace."

Salvador   Spanish version of Salvatore.

Salvatore   Italian origin from Latin meaning "savior" or "helper." Other forms include Sal, Salvador, Salvidor.

Sam, Sammy, Sammie   Diminutives of Samuel and Samson.

Samson   Hebrew origin (Biblical) meaning "sun." Other forms include Sam, Sammie, Sammy, Sampson, Sanson.

Samuel   Hebrew origin (Biblical) meaning "God heard." Other forms include Sam, Sammie, Sammy, Samuele.

Sander, Sanders   Variations of Alexander.

Sandy   Diminutive of Alexander or Sanford.

Sanford   Old English origin meaning "of the crossing of the sandy river."

Sargent   Old French origin meaning "officer of the army."

Sasha, Sascha, Sacha   Russian diminutives of Alexander.

Saul   Hebrew origin (Biblical) meaning "asked for." Other forms include Sol, Solly, Zollie.

Saxon   Old German origin meaning "man of the sword."

Schuyler   Dutch origin meaning "shielding."

Scot, Scott   Old English origin meaning "a man from Scotland." Other forms include Scotti, Scottie, Scotty.

Seamus   Irish version of James.

Sean   Irish version of John. Other forms include Shane, Shaun, Shawn.

Seaton   Old English origin meaning "town near the sea."

Sebastian   Latin origin meaning "from Sebastia." Other forms include Bastian, Bastien, Sebastiano, Sebastien.

89

Segel   Hebrew origin meaning "thing of great value."

Selah   Hebrew origin (Biblical) of uncertain derivation possibly meaning "musical interval."

Selden, Seldon   Old English origin meaning "of the estate valley."

Selig   Old German origin meaning "blessed." Alternate form: Zelig.

Septimus   Latin origin meaning "seventh."

Sergio, Serge   Italian and French versions of Latin origin meaning "one who serves."

Seth   Hebrew origin meaning "appointed."

Seward   Old English origin meaning "victory at sea."

Seymour   Old French origin meaning "man from St. Maur." Other forms include Morey, Morrie, Morry. See, Si, Sy.

Shalom   Hebrew origin meaning "peace." Other forms include Shlomo, Sholomo, Sholom.

Shamir   Hebrew origin (Biblical) meaning "substance harder than a rock."

Shamus   Irish version of John.

Shane   Irish version of John. Other forms include Shaine, Shayn, Shayne.

Shannon   Hebrew origin meaning "secure." Also Irish origin meaning "little wise one." Other forms include Shanan, Shaanon, Shanon, Shannan.

Shaw   Old English origin meaning "from the woods."

Shawn, Shaun   Variations of Sean.

Sheffield   Old English origin meaning "from the winding field."

Sheldon   Old English origin meaning "farm on the hill."

Shelley   Old German origin meaning "island of shells." Other forms include Shell, Shelly, Shellie.

Shelton   Old English origin meaning "town on a hill."

Shem   Hebrew origin (Biblical) meaning "name."

Shepherd   Old English origin meaning "shepherd."

Sherman   Old English origin meaning "one who shears." Other forms include Mannie, Manny, Sherm, Shermie.

Sherwood   Old English origin meaning "forest."

Si   Diminutive of Simon, Sidney, Seymour, etc.

Sid, Syd   Diminutives of Sidney.

Sidney, Sydney   Old French origin meaning "man from St. Denis."

Siegfried   Old German origin meaning "victory of peace." Other forms include Sig, Siggie, Siggy, Sigfried.

Sigmund   Old German origin meaning "shielding protector."

Silas   English version of Sylvester.

Silvester   See Sylvester.

Simcha, Simha   Hebrew origin meaning "joy."

Simon, Simeon   Hebrew origin (Biblical) meaning "one who hears." Other forms include Si, Sim, Sy, Syman, Symon.

Sinclair   Latin origin meaning "brightly shining."

Sion   Welsh version of John.

Sloan   Irish origin meaning "man of battle." Alternate form: Sloane.

Smith   Old English origin meaning "blacksmith." Other forms include Smittie, Smitty.

Sol   Diminutive of Solomon. Also an alternate form of Saul.

Solomon   Hebrew origin (Biblical) meaning "peace."

Sonny   Popular male nickname.

Spencer   Middle English origin meaning "administrator" or "one who dispenses." Other forms include Spence, Spense, Spenser.

Stacy   Greek origin meaning "reborn." Other forms include Stace, Stacey.

Stafford   English origin meaning "from the landing place near the river."

Stan   Diminutive of Stanley, Stanford, Stanislaus, etc.

Stanford   English origin meaning "from the stone ford."

Stanislaus   Scandinavian origin meaning "camp of glory."

Stanley   Old English origin meaning "rocky clearing."

Stanton   Old English origin meaning "from the stony town."

Stefan   German, Russian and Swedish version of Stephen.

Stephen   Greek origin meaning "crown." Other forms include Esteban, Etienne, Estevan, Stefan, Stefano, Steve, Steven, Stevie, Stevy.

Sterling, Stirling   English origin meaning "thing of great value."

Steve   Diminutive of Stephen, Steven.

Steven   English version of Stephen.

Stewart   See Stuart.

Stuart   Old English origin meaning "protector" or "steward." Other forms include Steward, Stewart, Stu.

Sullivan   Irish origin meaning "with the eyes of a hawk."

Sumner   Latin origin meaning "messenger."

Sven   Scandinavian origin meaning "young man."

Sy   Diminutive of Sylvester, Simon, Seymour, etc.

Sylvan   Variation of Sylvester.

Sylvester, Silvester   Latin origin meaning "woods" or "forest."

T

Tad   Diminutive of Thaddeus.

Talia   Arabic origin meaning "baby lamb."

Tamir   Hebrew origin meaning "tall and stately."

Tanner   Old English origin meaning "tanner."

Tate   Middle English origin meaning "one of great cheer."

Tavi   Aramaic origin meaning "the good one."

Taylor   Middle English origin meaning "tailor."

Ted, Teddy   Diminutive of Edward, Theodore, etc.

Telford   Old French origin meaning "iron cutter" or "fearsome battler."

Tennessee   American state name used as first name.

Terence   Latin origin meaning "gracious" or "smooth." Other forms include Terrence, Terrance, Terrencio, Terry.

Terry   Diminutive of Terence.

Thaddeus   Greek origin meaning "courageous one." Other forms include Tad, Tadd, Tadeo, Thad, Tadio.

Thatcher   Old English origin meaning "one who thatches roofs."

Theo   Diminutive of Theodore, Theobald, etc.

Theobald   Old German origin meaning "prince of the people." Other forms include Thibaut, Thibaud, Tybalt.

Theodore   Greek origin meaning "God's gift." Other forms include Theo, Theodor, Ted, Tedd, Teddie, Teddy, Teodoro.

Theodoric   Old German origin meaning "people's ruler." Other forms include Derek, Dereck, Dirk, Ted, Teddy, Teddie, Theo.

Thomas   Aramaic and Hebrew origin (Biblical) meaning "twin." Other forms include Tom, Tomas, Tomaso, Tommie, Tommy.

Thompson   Old English origin meaning "Tom's son." Alternate form: Thomson.

Thor   Scandinavian origin, the name of the god of thunder.

Thornton   Old English origin meaning "from the town near the thorns."

Thurston   Scandinavian origin meaning "stone of Thor."

Tibon   Hebrew origin meaning "one who studies nature."

Tiger   Latin origin meaning "tiger."

Tilden   Old English origin meaning "from the valley that is fertile."

Tim, Timmie, Timmy   Diminutives of Timothy.

Timothy   Greek origin meaning "to the honor of God." Other forms include Timotheus, Tymothy.

Titus   Greek origin meaning "giant one."

Tobias   Hebrew origin (Biblical) meaning "the goodness of God." Other forms include Tobiah, Tobin, Tobit, Toby.

Toby   Diminutive of Tobias.

Todd, Tod   Old English origin meaning "one who hunts foxes."

Tom, Tommie, Tommy   Diminutives of Thomas.

Tony   Diminutive of Anthony.

Tov, Tovi   Hebrew origin meaning "good."

Townsend   Old English origin meaning "of the end of the town."

Tracy   Irish origin meaning "mighty in battle." Other forms include Tracey, Tracie.

Travis   Old French origin meaning "collector of tolls."

Trayton   Old English origin meaning "from the town near the trees."

Trent   From the name of an English river.

Trevor   Welsh and Old English origin meaning "home near the sea."

Tristan   See Tristram.

Tristram   Welsh origin meaning "one who makes a great noise." Other forms include Tris, Tristan.

Troy   Old French origin meaning "curly hair."

Truman   Old English origin meaning "man of truth." Honors United States President Harry S Truman.

Tucker   Old English origin meaning "one who tucks."

Tudor   Welsh version of Theodore.

Turner   Old English origin meaning "lathe worker."

Ty   Diminutive of Tyrone, Tyler, Tyson, etc.

Tyler   Old English origin meaning "tile maker." Alternate form: Tylor.

Tyrone   Greek origin meaning "ruler."

Tyrus   English version of Thor.

Tyson   French origin meaning "firebrand."

U

Udell, Udall   Old English origin meaning "valley of yew trees."

Ulric, Ulrick   Old English origin meaning "having the power of a wolf." Other forms include Ulrich, Ric, Rick, Rickie, Ricky.

Ulysses   Latin and Greek origin meaning "angry."

Upton, Upten   Old English origin meaning "from up town" or "upper town."

Urban   Latin origin meaning "of the city."

Uriah   Hebrew origin (Biblical) meaning "my light is God." Other forms include Uri, Uriel, Yuri.

V

Val   Diminutive of Valentine.

Valentine   Latin origin meaning "strong." Other forms include Val, Valentino, Valentin.

Van, Vann   Dutch origin meaning "of." Also diminutives of Vance.

Vance   Old English origin meaning "by the marsh."

Vanya   Russian diminutive of John.

Vaughan   Welsh origin meaning "tiny."

Vered   Hebrew origin meaning "rose."

Verdun   French city name used as first name. Alternate form: Verdon.

Vern   Abbreviation of Verdon, Verdun, Vernon.

Vernon   French origin meaning "place of the alder tree."

Vic   Diminutive of Victor.

Victor   Latin origin meaning "victor." Other forms include Vic, Victoir, Vittorio.

Vincent   Latin origin meaning "conquering."

Vinny, Vinnie, Vince   Diminutives of Vincent.

Virgil   Latin origin meaning "bearer of the staff." Alternate form: Vergil.

Vito   Spanish and Latin origin meaning "vital" or "alive."

Vladimir   Russian origin meaning "ruler of great power."

W

Wade   Old English origin meaning "from the place where one can cross the river."

Wainwright   Old English origin meaning "builder of wagons." Other forms include Wain, Waine, Wayne, Wright.

Wakefield   Old English origin meaning "wet field."

Walden   Old English origin meaning "from the woods."

Waldo   Old German origin meaning "power."

Walker   Old English origin meaning "cleaner."

Wallace   Scottish origin meaning "man from Wales." Other forms include Wallie, Wally, Wallis, Welch, Welsh.

Wallis   See Wallace.

Wally, Wallie   Diminutive of Wallace, Walker, Walter, etc.

Walt   Diminutive of Walter.

Walter   Old German origin meaning "mighty in battle." Other forms include Wallie, Wally, Walt, Walther.

Walton   Old English origin meaning "from the walled settlement."

Ward   Old English origin meaning "protector."

Warner   English version of Warren.

Warren   Old German origin meaning "protector."

Washington   Honors the first President of the United States, George Washington.

Watkin   Variation of Walter.

Watson   Old English origin meaning "Wat's son."

Wayland   Old English origin meaning "from the land by the road."

Wayne   Old English origin meaning "wagon maker." See Wainwright. Other forms include Wain, Waine.

Webster, Webb   Old English origin meaning "one who weaves."

Wellington   Old English origin meaning "place of worship in the clearing."

Wells   Old English origin meaning "wells."

Wendell   Old German origin meaning "stranger." Alternate form: Wendel.

Werner   German version of Warner.

Wes   Diminutive of Wesley, Weston, etc.

Wesley   Old English origin meaning "west meadow."

Weston   Old English origin meaning "from the farm that faces west."

Wharton   Old English origin meaning "shore town."

Whitman   Old English origin meaning "man with the white hair."

Whitney   Old English origin meaning "from the white estate."

Whittaker   Old English origin meaning "white field."

Wilbur   Old German origin meaning "of special resolve." A version of Gilbert. Other forms include Wilbert, Wilburt.

Wilfred   Old German origin meaning "of peace." Other forms include Fred, Wilfrid, Will, Willie, Willy.

Wilhelm   German version of William.

Will   Diminutive of Wilfred, William, Willard, etc.

Willard   Old German origin meaning "very brave."

William   Old German origin meaning "brave protector" or "leader." Other forms include Bill, Billie, Billy, Wil, Will, Willie, Willy, Willis, Wilmer.

Willis   Form of William.

Wilmer   Form of William.

Wilson   Honors President of the United States Thomas Woodrow Wilson.

Win   Diminutive of Winston, Winfield, Winslow, etc.

Windsor   Old English origin meaning "bank of the river."

Winfield   Old English origin meaning "of the field of friendship."

Winslow   Old English origin meaning "of the hill of my friend."

Winston   Old English origin meaning "of firm friendship." Honors British Prime Minister Winston Churchill. Other forms include Win, Winn, Winnie, Winny, Wyn.

Winthrop   Old English origin meaning "friendly town."

Wolf   Old German origin meaning "wolf." Alternate form: Wolfe.

Wolfgang   Old German origin meaning "stride of the wolf."

Woodrow   Old English origin meaning "pass in the woods." Honors President of the United States Thomas Woodrow Wilson.

Woody, Woodie, Wood   Diminutives of Woodrow.

Wright   Old English origin meaning "carpenter."

Wyatt   Old French origin meaning "small battler."

Wyndham   Old English origin meaning "from the town near the curving road."

Wynn, Wynne   Welsh origin meaning "white."

X

Xavier   Arabic origin meaning "shining."

Xenos   Greek origin meaning "stranger."

Xerxes   Persian origin meaning "of royal blood" or "prince."

Y

Yaacov, Yaakov   Hebrew version of Jacob.

Yadin, Yadon   Hebrew origin (Biblical) meaning "judge."

Yale   Old English origin meaning "from the fertile part of the upper land."

Yancy   French and American Indian version of "Yankee" or "English man."

Yehuda, Yehudah   Hebrew version of Judah.

Yehudi   Hebrew origin meaning "praise."

Yigdal   Hebrew origin meaning "to grow large."

Yoel   Hebrew version of Joel.

Yoram   Hebrew origin meaning "the Lord is exalted."

Yule, Yul   Old English origin meaning "yuletide."

Yuri   Diminutive of Uriah, Uriel.

Yves   Old French origin meaning "archer." Other forms include Ives, Ivor.

Z

Zachariah Hebrew origin (Biblical) meaning "God remembers." Other forms: See Zachary.

Zachary Hebrew origin meaning "God remembers." Other forms include Zac, Zack, Zach, Zacharia, Zachariah, Zacharias, Zecharia, Zecharias, Zeke.

Zak, Zac, Zach Diminutes of Isaac, Zachariah, Zachary.

Zamir Hebrew origin meaning "nightingale."

Zane English version of John.

Zebadiah Hebrew origin meaning "God's gift."

Zebulun, Zeb Hebrew origin (Biblical) meaning "honoring."

Zedekiah Hebrew origin (Biblical) meaning "God is just."

Zeke Diminutive of Ezekiel, Zachary, Zachariah.

Zelig See Selig.

Zemer Hebrew origin meaning "song."

Zeviel Hebrew origin meaning "deer." Other forms include Zev, Zevi.

Zimri Hebrew origin (Biblical) meaning "rejoice with song."

Zion Hebrew origin meaning "sign."